The Future of Our Schools

The Future
of Our Schools

Teachers Unions
and Social Justice

Lois Weiner

Haymarket Books
Chicago, Illinois

Published by
Haymarket Books
P.O. Box 180165, Chicago, IL 60618
773-583-7884
info@haymarketbooks.org
www.haymarketbooks.org

ISBN: 978-1-60846-262-9

Trade distribution:
In the US through Consortium Book Sales and Distribution,
www.cbsd.com
In the UK, Turnaround Publisher Services, www.turnaround-uk.com
In Canada, Publishers Group Canada, www.pgcbooks.ca
In Australia, Palgrave Macmillan, www.palgravemacmillan.com.au
All other countries, Publishers Group Worldwide, www.pgw.com

Special discounts are available for bulk purchases by organizations
and institutions. Please contact Haymarket Books for more information
at 773-583-7884 or info@haymarketbooks.org.

This book was published with the generous support of the Wallace Global
Fund and Lannan Foundation.

Printed in Canada by union labor on recycled paper containing 100
percent postconsumer waste in accordance with the Green Press Initiative,
www.greenpressinitiative.org.

Library of Congress CIP data is available.

1 3 5 7 9 10 8 6 4 2

Contents

To George and Gladys Weiner, my first teachers, from whom I learned to speak out for social justice

Part
One

1.

Understanding the Assault on Public Education

Throughout the world, teachers, parents, and students are experiencing wrenching changes in how schools are run, who teaches, and what may be taught. Students are being robbed of meaningful learning, of time for play or creativity—for anything that's not tested. Hostile politicians blame teachers for an astounding list of social and economic problems ranging from unemployment to moral decline. In all but the wealthiest school systems, academic accomplishment has been reduced to scores on standardized tests that for-profit companies develop and evaluate. Parents, citizens, teachers, and students—education's most important stakeholders— have little say about what is taught, while corporate chiefs, politicians in their thrall, and foundations that receive funding from billionaires who profit from pro-business education policies determine who teaches and how. Children from affluent families face intensified competition for high grades, high SAT scores, a resume that will ease passage into a prestigious college and a well-paid career. Children whose parents have little formal education and who attend under-resourced schools experience intense pressures to succeed on standardized tests and school days that consist mostly of test preparation. I've written this book for teachers who are committed to social justice and democracy, in our society and in our schools. From my work with teachers and college students who want to teach, I see the hope and idealism this new generation brings. Most teachers I work with focus on making change through their teaching. They consider what they do in the classroom the way to change the world. Another group of teachers and school professionals, often those who work with immigrant students and teachers of color who have gone into teaching to be of service to the communities in which they live, see themselves as advocates for students, families, and communities that experience prejudice and limited social opportunity. And I'm seeing more and more teachers who want to make their unions more democratic, proactive, and militant. I've also observed that these three groups of teachers often don't collaborate and may not see one another as allies. One goal of this book is to explain why it's essential to create a movement that brings these groups together and how that might be done.

While we have to understand the powerful forces arrayed against us, we also need to keep in mind that every major improvement to education occurred because social movements—ordinary people banding together to make change—made others see issues differently. We can reverse the assault on public education if we create a new social movement of teachers that knows how to learn from and work with parents, communities, activists on other social issues, and other labor unions.

A Global Project Transforming Public Education in Ways the Rich and Powerful Dictate

It may seem as though many policies, like closing schools that have low test scores, are irrational or just ignorant. Politicians' lack of knowledge about education and animus toward teachers are both factors, but a far more onerous, chilling agenda drives the collection of policies destroying public education as it has existed for more than a century. The rhetoric of improving educational opportunity for those who have been excluded from prosperity has been used throughout the world to defend transformation of schooling that amounts to destroying what has existed for a century, to make drastic alterations in what is taught, how schools are funded and run, and who teaches.

We need—always—to introduce criticisms of the current reforms by affirming an unequivocal recognition of inequality, current and historic, and of our commitment to providing all children with a high-quality education. At the same time, we confront the reality that policies that are touted to "put children first" and "make services work for poor people" actually increase inequality for the vast majority of children who most need improved schools. Sometimes I am told that such a vast, well-organized project could not exist without the US public knowing more about it and that what I am describing sounds like a conspiracy.[1] Conspiracies are, by definition, secret. Yet the global project of wealthy, powerful elites to transform education has been quite public for more than a quarter century. Alas, we in the global North have been wearing blinders for decades. Evidence about the real aims and actual effects of "free market" reforms has been available for decades—if we looked in the right places, that is, at prospectuses from corporations developing new products and reports from the World Bank. The record is quite clear that lofty-sounding slogans mask the drive of transnational corporations to refashion education to fit their vision of a new global economy. For the elites who control corporations, media, and government, public expenditure on educating workers beyond the skill level needed for low-paying jobs is wasted. Since most jobs being created require no more than an eighth-grade education (think of Walmart's "associates"), only a handful of people need to acquire the sophisticated thinking and skills to manage and control the world's productive resources. Minimally educated workers need only minimally educated teachers. Oversight of lowered expectations for educational outcomes can be achieved through the use of standardized testing. Therefore, a well-educated (and well-paid) teaching force, it is argued by elites establishing educational policy, is a waste of scarce public money.[2]

Financial and political elites, working through international organizations, like the World Bank and the International Monetary Fund, began this project forty years ago when they imposed school reform on countries in Latin America, Africa, and Asia as a quid pro quo for economic aid. The project was first introduced in Chile, under Pinochet's brutal military dictatorship (supported by the United States), when schooling was privatized under the tutelage of Milton Friedman.[3] The project has emerged differently in the more industrially developed nations and though specifics of this social engineering differ in significant ways from one country to another, the same footprint is recognizable. Make public education a "free market" open to entrepreneurs; create a revolving door of minimally trained teachers; reduce the curriculum to basic math and literacy content that workers will need to compete for low-paid jobs; control teachers and students with standardized testing; and weaken public oversight by breaking up school systems and replacing them with privately operated schools.

In much of the world this framework of "free market" policies is called "neoliberalism," a term unfamiliar in the United States. This new term signifies a key shift in the thinking of elites that control the world's resources—and governments. In the United States, "liberalism" is associated with development of the welfare state, government policies like Franklin D. Roosevelt's New Deal, and Lyndon Johnson's Great Society. The term "neoliberalism" refers to quite a different political stance, drawing on the ideas of the first liberals (like Adam Smith), who developed theories about how "free markets" operate.[4] I am often asked about the intentions of the individuals who support neoliberal reforms, especially politicians who may identify themselves as liberals or progressives. Are they misguided? Ignorant? I think since we can't know what's going on inside of someone's head, there's little benefit in focusing on intentions. Instead we should examine ideology.

As with "neoliberalism," "ideology" is a term that can be confusing to people in the United States. Other economic and political systems have ideologies, but not us in the United States—right? If we use "ideology" to mean shared political beliefs about how a society operates, its spoken and unspoken rules, then every society has a dominant ideology to explain why its political and economic systems are good and fair. Analyzing ideology rather than intentions helps explain why people who seem to care, genuinely, about poor kids embrace reforms that do harm. They buy into neoliberal ideology, primarily the belief that the "free market" and "choice" will solve the problem of educational inequality.

Persistent inequality, in society and education, is at the heart of neoliberalism's appeal, not only to the wealthy but also to many poor and working people. Public education in the United States has not, historically, served poor and working people as well as it should, and we need to acknowledge that in order for our case about what's wrong with current "deforms" to be credible to people who should be our allies. We also have to be forthright in stating that while teachers and their unions did not create educational inequality, they have been too complicitous in maintaining it, from the very start of mass public education.[5] On the other hand, many policies in the '60s and '70s that could not have been enacted without support from teachers, teachers unions, and organized labor did, in fact, help reduce inequality in school outcomes. One example is high-quality early childhood education. Another is school lunch programs. At the same time that we note the successes, it's essential to understand that much more was needed. Some of the '60s reforms were, in hindsight, problematic, like using standardized test scores to measure whether federal money was well spent. This history shows us that education cannot on its own reverse deeply rooted causes of school failure, like poverty, racism, and unemployment, but schools and teachers that are better supported can make strides in closing the gap.[6]

Teachers Unions and Social Justice: Making the Connections Real

There's far more to neoliberalism's global assault on teachers and teachers unions than I can summarize in this book. However, teachers committed to working for social justice need to understand a few key issues. The neoliberal project in education has generated opposition wherever teachers and parents have the political freedom to resist—and in some places where they do not. The architects of this project aim to eliminate spaces in schools for critique, social justice teaching, and voices of parents and community—that is, when the voices are not a chorus supporting neoliberal goals. The elites who are orchestrating school "deform" understand (unfortunately, more than do most teachers) that despite their all-too-glaring problems, teachers unions are the main impediment to the neoliberal project being fully realized. Even when unions don't live up to their ideals, teacher unionism's principles of collective action and solidarity contradict neoliberalism's key premises—individual initiative and competition. Neoliberalism pushes a "survival of the fittest" thinking. Labor unions presume people have to work together to protect their common interests.

Unions press for *collective* voice and intervention to counter the employer's absolute control. Working together, employees possess a strength much greater than they have as individuals. Without a union, employees have no protection and no rights except those the employer grants. Especially in an occupation like teaching in which there is so much disagreement about what constitutes ideal practice, a supervisor has tremendous power to decide whether an individual is doing the job well. At its best the union brings individuals together to create a collective definition of professional conduct and responsibilities.

Another reason unions are a threat is that they can exercise *institutional* power. As organizations they have legal rights. Because unions have institutional roots, they are a stable force. And a union is able to draw on a regular source of income, membership dues.

These characteristics give teachers unions an organizational capacity seldom acquired by advocacy groups or parents, who generally graduate from activity in schools along with their children.

I know from my work as a teacher educator that what I've written about the unions' potential is often a hard sell to teachers and parents, so I want to clarify that I am explaining what gives unions their potential strength, not excusing what they don't do or do wrong. It's important to say, loudly, that the potential of teachers unions is not being realized and that they need to be transformed. Often union officials tell reformers not to "wash our dirty linen in public." However, this dirty laundry has already been paraded to great advantage by our enemies. The only way we will persuade teachers and the public that unions can be different—better—is by coming clean about problems.

The very factors that make unions stable and potentially powerful also induce bureaucracy and conservatism. Consider the difference between how principals and superintendents are chosen and the elections that must occur in unions. Teachers unions are membership organizations, "owned" by their members, whose votes keep the leadership in power and whose dues keep the organization operating. Yet neither unions as organizations nor union members as individuals are immune to prejudices that infect a society, even when these prejudices contradict the union's premises of equality in the workplace. The automatic collection of dues from members' paycheck stabilizes the union financially but also insulates officers from members' disgruntlement. Contracts offer protection, but they are very complex documents, and the staff's specialized knowledge and skills in negotiating and enforcing contracts can encourage members' passivity. When the law gives a union the right to negotiate a contract, it also generally gives the union exclusive bargaining rights, meaning that members can't replace their union with another one they think will be more responsive, at least not during the life of the contract.

Classrooms, teachers, and unions are affected by social, economic, and political life. The Right has become bolder and government policies more conservative in almost every realm. The communities we work with have been altered too, by more economic hardship and political repression. We must also acknowledge our opponents' ideological victories in changing how people think about education and government. The social movements that support social justice teaching and union work are weaker now. When I started teaching, we could often use school resources to support social justice work. For instance, when I was chair of my union local's women's rights committee, I helped organize a professional development conference that involved the women's studies program at a local university, along with community groups.

Today, in contrast, teachers and teachers unions have fewer allies and are in many ways more politically isolated. Many teachers in schools struggling with low test scores fear their schools will be shut down. Others, in schools that seem immune from being closed, shut their classroom doors, literally and figuratively, trying to deny the powerful social and political forces that are subverting their hard work with students. Too many teachers have stopped asking, "Is this good for our kids?" because they fear that questioning authority puts their jobs at risk.

The deterioration in teachers' confidence to stand up for their students, for social justice, and for their dignity as workers mirrors the weakening of teachers unions. If you care about social justice in education, you have a very important stake in not only the continued existence of teachers unions but also in their transformation. Though the popular media cast teachers unions as powerful, the unions are quite weak where it counts most, at the school site. Union leaders are disoriented and confused. When I started teaching, teachers unions might win economic gains without doing much to mobilize members. That is no longer the case. The propaganda campaign we have experienced has achieved its goal of discrediting the unions as organizations and even the idea of teacher unionism among much of the public and teachers as well. Yet we need democratic, vibrant, progressive teachers unions to turn back privatization of schools, which spells destruction for public education. To stand up as individuals for our dignity and our students' well-being, we need the institutional support a good union can provide. If we fail to make the unions what they should be, most students in our country—and the world—will be trained for a life of menial labor, poverty, or imprisonment.

What I've explained so far points to why we need to take back the unions. At the same time, activists who focus their attention on the teachers unions need the vision of teachers whose paramount concern is what goes on in their classrooms. Because of the conservatizing factors I've mentioned in this chapter, as well as others I explain later in the book, even progressive unions and radical teacher union leaders feel pressure to narrow the union's focus, to take up "bread and butter" issues that are more popular with many members than social justice concerns. For teachers to succeed in pushing back on school closings, standardized testing, and a narrowed curriculum, they must also have strong, mutually respectful alliances with communities and parents. School workers who have roots in minority communities are a key resource, and are often overlooked. Sometimes these individuals work as aides and teachers in bilingual or English as a Second Language programs. In some districts, workers who belong to another union can provide crucial personal links with community activists and parents.

As attacks on teachers unions have intensified in the past few years, I've been asked by teachers for practical reading about how to improve their unions. Finding no book that I could recommend, I've written this one. In developing my ideas for this book, I've drawn on my work as a researcher, teacher union activist, professor of education, and career high school teacher. To make the book more readable, I've tried to keep references to the absolute minimum. For current updates on research and analysis on teachers unions, you may want to refer to my website.[7] All royalties from this book will go to Teachers Unite, an organization that I think embodies the goals of building a movement of teachers, parents, and community activists committed to social justice in education and social movement teacher unionism.

The second section of this book contains articles I've written over the past thirty years for *New Politics*. This material provides additional background about issues that deserve more attention than I could give in this book, which I conceive of as an intelligent activist's guide to the teacher union universe.

One final note: I often use the word "teacher" to signify members of teachers unions, but I acknowledge in advance that the label is misleading. Teachers unions usually represent constituencies other than K–12 teachers with their own classrooms, including social workers, paraprofessionals, psychologists, librarians, adult school teachers, and substitute teachers. A strong, democratic union values each constituency's unique contribution and takes care to demonstrate to all members that it is a union of equals.

2.

Protecting the Heart of Teaching

Our responsibility to do right by our students is at the heart of teaching. Under the present conditions in many schools and most school systems, teachers are pressured to carry out mandates that actually harm kids. Though some teachers manage to protect their students from test-prep mania and other destructive policies, many more lack the skill, confidence, and courage to resist as individuals. I think teachers can no longer presume that if they shut their classroom doors and concentrate all their energies on what goes on in their classrooms, they are satisfying their moral charge. While our first responsibility is always to our students, teachers need to open their classroom doors, literally and figuratively, enlarging the definition of the workspace to include the school and community.

To be clear, I am not saying we should expect every teacher to become a political activist—though we'd certainly be in better shape to defend public education if many more were. What I am proposing is thinking about how to politicize teachers who do not understand why the world outside their classroom has to be a consideration for the decisions they make in their work lives, as well as encouraging teachers who are already more politically aware to become more active. For instance, I know several teachers who are adamant about insulating themselves (and their students) from negative influences in their schools, who were receptive to my suggestion that being true to their professional obligations meant informing parents of their English as a Second Language (ESL) students about cutbacks in ESL services. Other teachers may be politicized through work informing parents about the harm done by standardized testing, a project the British Columbia Teachers Federation undertook.[1] An encouraging sign of teachers' increasing politicization is the growth of local organizations of social justice teachers that hold conferences, study groups, and projects to encourage social justice teaching.[2]

To create a new social movement of teachers who understand what's at stake in protecting teaching's moral core, and who are passionate about social justice, we need new spaces that bring teachers in varying degrees of politicization together. We need to support the development of networks that emerge naturally when social movements are more robust than they are at this historical moment.

New Territory and New Rules

In fall 2011 the Occupy Wall Street movement and its local offshoots have excited hope of reversing the control of the 1 percent and helped to create space for resistance. Yet today's struggle occurs on a landscape that was unimaginable forty years ago. Richard Nixon signed laws protecting the environment, civil rights, and labor that all but the most liberal Democrats today dismiss as too

costly, intrusive, or radical. Vast changes have been made to education, and parents, teachers, and even seasoned school activists are
often not sure what to believe. Neoliberal rhetoric about "putting
children first," ahead of purportedly selfish school employees and
their unions, may seem to make sense, even if parents don't see self-
ishness in their children's teachers. Nonprofit organizations and
foundations do the work of right-wing think tanks pushing for privatization and profits.[3] Often citizens and parents who see through
the propaganda and oppose making schools into profit centers for
corporations feel helpless to stop these policies. Parents who experience the reforms' damage firsthand often feel they are powerless
to act. Elected officials, from school boards to governors, break the
law with impunity. Take the governor of New Jersey (please!), who
proclaimed that his crusade to save New Jersey's children justified
his defying the State Supreme Court's orders to give the state's low-
income school districts the funding to which they were legally en-
titled. Democrats and Republicans excuse violating union contracts
or firing teachers wholesale from schools and districts with the rationale that they are saving children's lives.

Another change is the labor movement's diminished power. The
percentage of workers who are in unions has fallen—dramatically.
Public education is the only sector of the economy that is still heavily
unionized, and many teachers, especially those who come through
"fast track" certification programs and worked in the private sector
where unionization is negligible, may be unfamiliar with unions or
even scared by them. Also, teachers unions' traditional allies, including civil rights organizations and community-based groups, can no
longer be counted as automatic supporters. Traditions of solidarity
within the labor movement are weak, although they are being revived,

as we saw in the inspiring struggle of Wisconsin's teachers and public employees. Still, the reelection of Wisconsin's governor also illustrates the pitfalls that face teachers and other public employees if they play by the old rules. We will not be able to defend education if we rely on the same strategies that unions have been using for the past twenty years, especially looking to "friends" in the Democratic Party.[4]

Neoliberal think tanks and foundations, like the American Enterprise Institute, the Broad Foundation, and the Gates Foundation, have recruited people identified by the popular media as spokespeople for oppressed groups. When the Reverend Al Sharpton joined former New York City Schools chancellor Joel Klein, Newt Gingrich, and Arne Duncan to campaign for Barack Obama's "Race to the Top" legislation, the alliance was big news. What didn't get the same attention in the media was the half-million-dollar grant to Sharpton's organization from a hedge fund headed by another former New York City Schools chancellor, Harold Levy.[5] Who these people touted as community leaders really represent is never clear, but their endorsement of policies like charter schools, behind the smokescreen of educational equity, adds to the public perception that the reforms have the support of minority parents—and that teachers who oppose the changes are blocking real improvement.

At the same time, teaching has become more demanding than it was just a few years ago, due to larger class sizes, cuts in support services, and more autocratic administration. Working with young people is harder because of the social devastation caused by unemployment and increased poverty. Teachers are worried, tired, and often frightened. They have been influenced by the masterful anti–teacher union propaganda orchestrated by right-wing think tanks, foundations, corporations, and supposedly nonpartisan "watchdog" organizations. Lots of teachers are confused about merit pay, particularly those who see themselves as especially conscientious or committed in ways other teachers are not to helping students, families, and communities of color. The challenges are substantial and our resources limited, so we have to be strategic—meaning being clear—about our goals.

Putting School Reform and Teacher Quality in Perspective

We need to be upfront that in some schools and classrooms students are not being treated respectfully or educated well. Sometimes teachers who work in schools would not want to send their children to the schools in which they teach. We have to find ways to put this on the table so that we maintain credibility with our natural allies—parents and activists in communities that have, historically, not been given equal educational opportunity. Improving educational outcomes for kids whose families are poor and whose neighborhoods are dangerous will take a great deal more than improving teaching. While not all teachers are great (who is, in any occupation?), we need to make the case that the exclusive focus on teacher quality ignores many powerful social factors outside the classroom.[6] Consider how little we hear about child hunger, homelessness, and unemployment affecting school achievement, especially in comparison to the horror tales about tenure and union contracts. As experienced teachers know, what occurs in classrooms also depends on how well schools are run, on the quality of the administrators who oversee the school's operations, set the school's tone, and supervise teachers.

Still, I cringe when teachers and union officials answer tirades about poor teaching with the argument that schools and teachers are helpless in light of social problems. Worse still is criticism that parents aren't doing their jobs so teachers can't do theirs. This stance of denial falls into our enemies' trap of making us seem uncaring and self-serving. It isolates us from parents, whom we need on our side. Moreover, blaming parents or saying that schools are helpless to do a better job ignores that some schools do better than others. There are ways we can improve schools, and a teachers union's mantra should be that social and economic facts influence what occurs in classrooms, *and*, at the same time, schools and teachers will have better results when they are better supported. I'd say that *The Schools Chicago Students Deserve*, a report published by the Chicago Teachers Union, is a fine model of how to set out what we need to make schools work.[7] The report describes the services and rich instructional diet all kids deserve and at the same time explains how race and economic status configure the low-quality education that poor kids of color actually receive.

Education can't solve the country's economic problems or create new jobs, and we must say so loudly. By insisting that education is the key to ending poverty, politicians avoid taking on the fight for economic policies the country desperately needs. Labor and progressives need to push hard on the federal government to create jobs that benefit the public and pay enough for families to live decently.[8] Schools (and teachers) can help put all students on an equal educational footing for existing jobs. Better schools can democratize the competition for jobs, but they can't eliminate the "tyranny of the labor market," the absence of enough well-paying jobs.[9] Good teachers unions will join with other labor unions in fighting for full employment, as was done during the Great Depression. But teachers unions have special responsibilities, too.

What Makes a Union of Teachers Different?

What makes a union of teachers different from a union of bus drivers, electricians, or nurses? Describing teaching as a profession is often an opener for arguing that what we need are professional organizations, not labor unions, but we can't let that deter us from examining this issue because the unique nature of teachers' work is one of the reasons teachers are experiencing such a vicious political attack.

To start, we should be clear about the ways unions of teachers are, or should be, like other good labor unions. First, all labor unions should be defining their members' interests broadly, seeing members' immediate interests as inseparable from what's best for working people. Second, workers in public service and the unions that represent them have to be especially mindful of championing quality services, especially for people who have traditionally been underserved.

In one respect, teachers are no different from other workers in needing democratic, vibrant unions that stand up for social justice. But a good teachers union has special moral and political responsibilities because of the unique nature of teachers' work. Teachers are idea workers. We need to be absolutely clear about this aspect of our work because it's a major reason the banks and corporations aim to control teaching and teachers. A key aim of the neoliberal project, that is, the goal of the educational policy being pushed by the 1 percent and their political allies, is to destroy teachers' autonomy and the space this creates in schools for critical thought and for ideas of freedom and social justice.

Most teachers don't think of themselves as "idea workers." They enter the profession because they love being with children or the subject matter they want to teach. Teachers think about what went on in class today and what they will do tomorrow, next week, and maybe next month. They often don't consider that in their classrooms they are, in fact, shaping society. Unfortunately, the architects of attacks on teachers understand all too well that regardless of a teacher's conscious intent, s/he influences how students see themselves and society. Teachers have the potential to affect social arrangements, challenging the authority of elites who have an interest in maintaining their own power and privilege. While all labor unions—all citizens!—have a stake in promoting and protecting teachers' ability to educate students who can think for themselves, a union of teachers has a particular responsibility to safeguard teachers' rights to help students think critically. Protecting teachers' academic freedom is one of the union's most essential tasks. That means fighting for tenure and the guarantee of due process when complaints are made about teachers' professional conduct.

However, another aspect of teachers' work complicates the union's defense of academic freedom and its members' performance. Teachers are morally and legally responsible for children's well-being. Laws requiring children's compulsory attendance at school make children captive in classrooms. When I say this to teachers, they are startled, and understandably so. They don't view their students as prisoners. However, it's critical for union activists to remember that students are indeed captive and if teachers are not doing their jobs well enough, students can be harmed. The union has an allegiance *both* to its members as workers *and* to the protection of students' well-being.

The unions have been pilloried in the media for protecting incompetents. As a result, union officials have tended to downplay the reasons for teachers' rights to hearings and due process. Given the ferocity of the attacks about bad teachers, union leaders' wariness is understandable. But it is also wrong and dangerous. What the unions should be saying is that we can't have a democratic society if we have undemocratic schools. Our society gives those accused of criminal acts the right to be considered innocent until proven guilty. People with whom we entrust our children should have the same protection. "Due process" requires only that a teacher accused of wrongdoing has the right to a fair, impartial hearing, based on evidence. There's no escape from making this case to the public (and union members), and the unions have to do so much more vigorously.

The other reason protection of due process is so important is that teachers must respond to different, often conflicting, rules and demands from supervisors. Often what is first publicized in the press as an open-and-shut case of teacher negligence turns out to be quite different, though the clarification is seldom given as much publicity as the original charge. The media's obsession with cases of teachers' malfeasance obscures everything that schools and school districts botch. In defending teachers' rights to due process, the union insists that schools take responsibility for factors over which teachers have no control.

I acknowledge that in light of the propaganda about the unions defending incompetent teachers, unions will not be popular in making my argument. It takes courage, but the task is inescapable. When anyone questions how the union can defend a teacher who has been accused of even the most egregious act, I think the first question is, how do you know s/he did it? How do you know your evidence is reliable? The follow-up is, if you were accused of a crime, should you have a right to present evidence in your defense? Doesn't s/he have this right? It may be that the allegation is so serious that the union leadership feels isolated from the members. In this case, the union may want to ask union representatives to discuss a policy, to come up with an alternative that protects due process and professional ideals. In my experience, when questions of impropriety or incompetence are brought to members, there is lively debate that ends in decisive support for protecting due process. People realize that they might be in a similar position and need to have the union stand up for them, so the discussion educates members about the importance of solidarity.

Teaching as Caring

Teaching well is described as an art, craft, and science, as well as a kind of caring, like parenting. Yet schools in the United States are organized in a way that undercuts teaching's complexity, especially its nurturing functions. For instance, a teacher's workday omits time for the work that supports instruction. No time is built in to the school day for teachers to confer with one another, meet with parents or students privately, plan, evaluate student work, complete documentation of attendance and achievement, and so on. Mostly teachers are expected to do all these things in the forty-five-minute preparation period they have, an alteration in the school day that was won by teachers unions in the 1960s and '70s.

Good teaching is personal. In one respect, we're like parents. I've heard this aspect of teaching denigrated as "babysitting," and though teachers unions need to respect members' varied—even contradictory—beliefs about what constitutes good teaching, I think defending teaching's nurturing functions is essential. Neoliberalism has succeeded in making many schools that serve children of working and poor families little more than training grounds for the factory—or prison. It's both morally essential and practical that teachers and unions stand up for children's human needs. The national teachers unions have yielded to neoliberalism's redefinition of schooling's purposes, away from development of our full human potential into job training. However, many parents look to schools to safeguard their children. It is parents, not bankers or the politicians they bankroll, who are the constituency we need to move to our way of viewing school reform. We are losing political ground because the unions have virtually surrendered the ideological battle about schooling's purposes. We need to project a different vision of what schools should be for everyone, not just teachers, as the Chicago Teachers Union has done in the proposal I mentioned previously.

The alternative vision has to counteract propaganda that teachers and teachers unions care only about themselves. The steady barrage of policies measuring and punishing teachers and students according to test scores is inseparable from neoliberalism's ideology of ruthless competition and individualism. It is this ideology we must turn back. An Australian researcher who has analyzed neoliberalism's success in casting social services, including schools, as profit centers proposes that we push back by insisting that schools be caring communities.[10] Rallying parents under the slogan "Make Schools Caring Communities—Not Factories," teachers and unions can infuse the elements of caring and collaboration into school organization and counter efforts to reduce schooling to job training. We will face a battle in making this argument to cynical reporters and hostile politicians. As I learned in talking with a newly elected union officer, he was battered in a press conference when he argued that the union didn't want teachers to compete against one another for merit pay. The cynical reporters scornfully dismissed his answer that good teaching was collaborative and that schools should be caring communities. He stuck to his guns in the press conference, as all union officials need to do. His answer was exactly right—and it is one that many parents and students want to hear from us. Our opponents may confuse idealism with naiveté, but we should not.

Especially in schools serving students who are marginalized in our society, school organization and regulations can be inhumane. Partly because contracts don't permit the union to bargain over nonmonetary issues, it's tempting for teachers unions to accept the school's structure and organization as a given. Yet the misfit between teaching as a human, nurturing activity and the school's rigid structure has a corrosive impact on teachers' morale and students' achievement. I realize that not all teachers welcome parent involvement, which can seem (and be) intrusive. But the union has to take leadership in working with parents and community—in coalitions, as equals—to take on the way schools are organized. Doing so is one of the keys to building successful alliances to counter neoliberalism's "solutions." Again, something that is a moral responsibility is also quite practical. We cannot expect parents to support us in economic struggles when we do not engage with them respectfully, as partners, in coalitions about their educational concerns.

Working with parents doesn't come naturally to most teachers or to union officers. Teachers often feel that parents, especially those who have little formal education, are hard to reach. It may surprise teachers to learn that low-income parents feel that teachers are hard to reach! Many parents who lack formal education and who don't measure up to the school's expectations are showing they care about their children's learning in ways that only teachers who have close personal connections to a community know firsthand. Researchers who interviewed African American mothers in a housing project learned that parents considered taking children to church every week a way to provide a sound moral base, which would translate into school success. However, the mothers wouldn't come to the school's "open house" to meet the teacher because they said it was not a priority when compared to other responsibilities as the breadwinner.

I often hear parents say that teachers don't care—and vice versa. This finger-pointing is counterproductive and ignores that schools were designed to be insular, cut off from communities and parents.[11] As a result, collaboration between parents and teachers (terms that mask the fact that the parent is usually a mom and the teacher is most often a woman) takes lots of time and commitment. Teachers and teachers unions have to struggle, consciously, not to acquire a bunker mentality. Tensions with parents are inescapable, especially when parents feel they are not respected by the union, as is often the case with groups who have experienced racial exclusion from labor unions. However, this is another hard issue there is no way to duck, as we learned from conflicts between black community activists and the mostly white teachers unions in the 1960s and '70s. Perhaps the most explosive of these conflicts occurred in Newark, New Jersey, in the early 1970s. In two bitter strikes the city was brought to the brink of race war, as the teachers union, though it was headed by an African American woman, and civil rights activists became increasingly blinded to the other side's justifiable desires for dignity and equality.[12] As I discuss in the article in *New Politics* reviewing a book on the strikes (reproduced as chapter 9 in this book), the racial divide was never healed, which made the city ripe for one of the most audacious campaigns for privatization, led by an African American, Democratic mayor and paid for by billionaire patrons. To bridge the racial divide, teachers unions must develop a race-conscious culture and vocabulary. Having officers and activists who are members of minority groups is a vital part of this process, but as was demonstrated in the Newark strikes, it is not sufficient. The unions have to nurture a culture in which race and racism are critiqued, frankly. This process can strengthen the union internally and at the same time shows parents and activists that the union is an ally that can be trusted. Building alliances that are mutually respectful is hard work, but as we have seen in Chicago, it can be done.

Professionally Speaking

I should clarify that although "professional" often connotes work that has an elevated social status, I'm using it to mean that someone meets the accepted standards of excellence in his/her occupation. To my knowledge, there's no word in English that comes closer to what I mean, and a conversation I overheard on a bus illustrates my definition. Many off-duty bus drivers ride this bus route to or from work, and I eavesdropped as my driver and his pal criticized another driver's cursing at abusive riders. "That's just so unprofessional!" my driver exclaimed. His colleague nodded vigorously in agreement. "It sure is," he said. "Very unprofessional."

What should be the union's role in teachers' exercise of their professional responsibilities, in particular when teachers develop curricula, decide on textbooks, consult on an instructional package? I think when teachers are functioning professionally as "idea workers" as they are when they decide what will be taught and how, the union should use its clout to try to create a vehicle in the school, separate from the union, for this work.

If teachers have a good union, do they also need separate space to pursue their responsibilities as "idea workers"? The first teachers union in the United States, formed by elementary schoolteachers in Chicago at the turn of the nineteenth century, thought so and pursued the creation of "teachers councils." These councils were similar in their function to a college or university faculty senate. They were organizationally independent of the union. The union's involvement was in advocating for creating the councils and pressing for council decisions to be taken seriously. Teachers elected representatives to the councils, which had an advisory role on educational decisions.[13]

When I began to teach in New York City, I saw the importance of having separate professional organizations and teachers unions. In California, the state teachers unions and professional associations collaborated on legislative matters, and a stellar English teacher was an officer of both the California Federation of Teachers and the California Association of Teachers of English. However, the organizations retained total organizational independence and sometimes came down differently on issues of curriculum. Quite a different situation existed in New York City, where the union's subject matter committees used the union's political clout to represent the union as speaking for teachers in regard to city and state decisions on curriculum and instruction. The subject committees blocked proposals that the union leadership found politically objectionable.

We need to maintain a separation between teachers being organized professionally as "idea workers" and the union's apparatus so as to protect teachers' freedom to advocate ideas that the union, even a good union, may find objectionable. We see the kind of separation I'm advocating in colleges and universities that are unionized and have a senate, which oversees curriculum. While the faculty union may be involved in decisions that relate to instruction, for instance in pressing the administration to lower class sizes, the two spheres are separate. This separation is especially important in K–12 schools because of the diversity of opinion among thoughtful teachers and parents about what works best in classrooms.[14] Teachers who are closer to minority and immigrant communities bring perspectives that their colleagues and the unions have to hear.[15] The union's responsibility is to protect the space for teachers, parents, and students to have those conversations.

Conventional (teachers union) wisdom has it that collective bargaining improved teachers' working conditions, and if we define teachers' work primarily in terms of wages and hours, that is accurate. In contrast, what's happened to teachers' influence on nonmonetary issues, like curriculum? One study argues that teachers in National Education Association (NEA) affiliates actually had more voice in professional matters before the NEA engaged in collective bargaining.[16] In part this occurred because collective bargaining laws defined the "scope of bargaining," what was legal to negotiate, quite narrowly. Most professional matters, like having a voice in adoption of materials or professional development, were ruled off-limits, leaving only class size, salary, and hours as bargaining concerns.

I think neoliberalism's success in painting unions as self-interested and selfish and the attack on the right to bargain contracts make this an opportune time to rethink the scope of bargaining. In other words, what do we get in legislation that gives us the right to negotiate legally binding contracts—as compared to what we give up? In California, I and other teacher union activists were advised by experts from the state and national unions to accept collective bargaining legislation with the usual narrow scope. We were persuaded that we would never get the legislation we wanted, but that we could at a later date modify the legislation (which has, to my knowledge, never occurred—anywhere) to cover professional concerns. Previous to having collective bargaining, my school district had school-site councils with department heads (elected, in the junior high and high schools) and grade-level leaders (elected, in the elementary schools). The councils met with principals, and while they were strictly advisory, in schools that had a strong union presence, the councils had considerable influence. Though we lacked the legal right to bargain collectively, teachers in my district could and did mobilize effectively to pressure the school board on salary and working conditions. With collective bargaining, we had a single bargaining agent and the right to have a contract. However, the councils lost their authority, and with their demise, teachers lost our collective voice about academic matters.

Because of this narrow scope of bargaining, teachers unions are generally precluded from addressing teachers' academic concerns, like standardized testing and textbook selection. One solution, which I develop in the next chapter, is for the unions to be remade, as social movements, and to reopen the question of how we will use the power of teachers.

3.

Building Social Movement Teachers Unions

The best way to explain what the union *should* be is to describe what it should *not* be, which is like most schools: hierarchical and paternalistic. Union members should feel confident that they set the union's key policies and direction. If union meetings consist of officers' monologues, if members are berated for not being active, if leaders respond defensively to suggestions about alternatives, if officers or staff act as if they call the shots, the union needs democratization.

Often union members assume someone else—anyone else— will run the union, and it will, somehow, continue to exist. Their perception and passivity are supported by the leadership's conception of the union. Perhaps without realizing it, members and leaders accept the "service model" of unionism that predominates in US labor. In this model, sometimes referred to as "business unionism," the union is run like a business and exists to provide services including lower rates for auto insurance; benefits from a welfare fund; pension advice; contract negotiations; and perhaps filing a grievance. Officers or staff make decisions on the members' behalf. The union as an organization functions based on the assumption (generally unarticulated, unless it's challenged) that paid officials know best about everything. They're supposedly the experts. Often they conduct negotiations in secret, reporting back only when a tentative agreement has been reached. Then members have the legal right to vote on whether the contract should be approved. But other than voting on a contract and electing officers every few years, members are passive. They are obliged only to pay dues and accept the leadership's expertise. Because the service model is predicated on members' reliance on the officers and staff, the union atrophies and the leadership evolves into a clique that is defensive and insular. Though the union constitution may provide ways for members to overturn officers' decisions, people are so uninvolved and uninformed that this right, existing in theory, is rarely exercised. Having been a union officer myself, I know that finding ways to mobilize members is very difficult. And without a clear understanding of why members' involvement is essential and knowledge of how to promote it, many well-intentioned leaders stop trying to reach out. Exclusionary ways of operating that are accepted out of what seems like necessity morph into principles. As I explain in the first chapter, the same factors that give unions their stability and strength make them prone to paternalism. One of the factors is the union's sense of purpose—how it sees its responsibilities and members' self-interest. In the service model, the union's goals are restricted to members' immediate economic concerns. The members' self-interest is defined very narrowly, as immediate "bread and butter" issues that can be negotiated in a contract. Politics is defined as electoral politics, not social justice. Electoral politics usually consists of deciding which Democrat to endorse, though sometimes a Republican is considered a "friend of labor" and wins the union's favor. Though US unions are barred by law from using members' dues for elections, the unions sponsor separate political organizations to which members can contribute as individuals, often by having contributions deducted from their paychecks. The union's involvement in community matters is often limited to donations to local charities, though during times when the union faces a hostile school board, friendly parents or community activists may be asked to sign a letter of support or make a speech at a school board meeting. Alliances with community groups, when they are formed, are limited to the "you scratch my back and I'll scratch yours" sort.[1]

Though dominant, business unionism is dangerously outdated. It undercuts teachers unions in effectively answering the charge that they are no different from other special interest groups, like for-profit operators of charter schools or companies producing testing materials. Though business unionism is touted as more efficient because officers and staff are experts, it is more than impractical. Given the horrific attacks on unions and teachers, business unionism is suicidal. No small group of officers, however intelligent or conscientious, can by themselves, or with the help of the dwindling number of politicians who support public education, substitute for the informed involvement of a mobilized membership. Democracy seems inefficient because it can be messy. Decisions take longer because more ideas and voices are involved in the process. However, the democratic process yields decisions that are often wiser, precisely because the problem has been seen from different, even contradictory perspectives. And in the end, the process generates decisions that will be more strongly defended—by more people.

The dissolution of the Philadelphia Public School District into "support networks" and the closure of its central office demonstrate that teachers unions have to reorganize, fast.[2] Their present organizational structure is obsolete. US politicians and the right-wing think tanks that are strategizing to "blow up" public school systems are succeeding.

A new movement of teachers can help spearhead development of the broad political and social resistance needed to reverse the tidal wave destroying public education, and social movement unionism is at the heart of that struggle. It is the alternative to the service or business model. A social movement union casts the union's strength as a function of its ability to mobilize its members to struggle on their own behalf. Union power comes from the bottom up, as it does in social movements. Union leaders offer direction and support for organizing, rather than telling members that their role is to let union officials set union policy. Just as important as the union's organizational form is its definition of the union's purpose. In social movement unions, members' self-interest is defined broadly, as much more than immediate economic and contractual concerns. The union struggles for its members' stake in a creating a more democratic, equitable society, and the union allies itself with other movements that are working for social justice, peace, and equality.

I use the term "social movement" union rather than "social justice" union, which may be more familiar to some readers, because I think "social movement" union addresses the need for unions' internal transformation, especially the need for union democracy. Social movement unionism gets at the relationship between the union's organization and its vision of social justice. A social movement union not only endorses social justice outside the school, it also exists as a social movement itself. One complaint leveled about social movement unionism is that it's not practical. It's argued that members' dues and officers' time should be devoted to immediate concerns, which are great enough to require twice the resources we can muster. I think we can see from history that when teachers unions act like their responsibility is limited to their members' immediate economic concerns, the unions end up taking positions that come back to haunt them. The union uses its resources to win a skirmish today, at the expense of building consensus with potential allies, whom it will need at a later date to win more important battles. A prime example is the terrible situation we face with health care. Because teachers unions (along with the rest of the labor movement) used their political power to obtain health care coverage for their members and didn't fight for universal health care such as exists in Canada and Western Europe, politicians have easily convinced taxpayers that teachers and other public employees should not have benefits that most voters lack. As a result, teachers have been isolated in trying to save their benefits, which have been drastically reduced. Fighting for the social good, which is what a social movement union does, is actually the more practical option. "Business union" thinking and operations are a self-deceptive indulgence we can't afford. A social movement teachers union builds agreement with its potential allies on educational issues by examining how potential allies view the problem and comes up with a consensus—before taking action.

Consider the difference in how a social movement union and a business union respond to school closings, "colocation" of charter schools in an existing building, or in the most drastic example yet, replacing the school district with networks of schools, most of them run by nonprofit groups that carry out the agenda of billionaires. The damage in privatizing schools, creating charter schools and charter school networks, is well documented.[3] Students and families are left to fend for themselves in finding alternative school placements, a process that often ends in academic failure. Experienced teachers, and even more often, experienced teachers of color, are put into pools of displaced teachers. Teachers unions have been incapable of stopping these school closings because the business union model assumes that union power consists of union officers' expertise to win concessions. In a business union, officers and staff may meet privately with the board and administration. A business union may contact local media. Maybe the union has a lawyer file suit on the grounds the closure violates the board policy or the union contract. But if union spokespeople try to cast their argument in terms of harm done to children by the school closures, the claim generally falls on deaf ears. Parents recall that in past struggles about school issues, the union's only intervention was to protect teachers' contractual rights.

In contrast, a social movement teachers union reaches out to its members, parents, students, and other school employees, as well as other unions that represent workers in the school. The teachers union takes leadership in organizing a coalition that looks at how to mobilize more support within the immediate neighborhood and the larger community, including other unions. What changes need to be made in the school to make it more successful? How can the union help win these from the board? The campaign to avoid the school closing begins with mobilizing parents and school employees in the school and is based on the principle that no decision of such importance should be made without consultation with those affected.

Campaigns of this sort in Los Angeles, Chicago, and Rochester have included demonstrations, packing board meetings for presentations, circulating petitions presented to the board and local politicians, and at times, civil disobedience, even occupying the school building. The protests are organized and publicized with social media, to counter the "news" in the corporate media, which seldom explains the harm done in school closings.

Social movement unionism requires stretching the union's definition of "what counts" for members. I often meet teachers who organize on political issues, like single-payer health care or immigrant rights, but say they can't participate in the union because they don't have time or don't find the union to be a congenial environment. If radical, politically conscious teachers don't help build a different kind of union, who will? I've had many discussions with union activists who find this situation frustrating and demoralizing. I share the frustration but try to keep in mind that the work teachers do on social justice outside the union helps to build a social movement union indirectly, by building public support for the political values and positions the union should endorse. For instance, antiwar organizers have told me that the peace movement has relied heavily on teachers' contributions of time and money, whereas the labor movement's support has been tepid, at best. We shouldn't counterpose union work to other political activity. Instead, we need to find ways for members to bring their activism *into* the union, encouraging them to use the union as a vehicle for social justice work. As the union becomes more open and more active, it generates a culture that is more inviting to teachers who haven't previously seen the union as a place they'd want to bring their political work. I saw this in the journey of an activist in anti-militarism work in schools who was invited by a new, progressive union leadership to join its (previously moribund) human rights committee—and bring the anti-military recruiting campaign with her. She had never cared about the union, but she energized the committee and while changing the union was changed herself. She explains that she learned the value of union work for the first time because she experienced its potential power. The union was able to develop a far more extensive campaign against military recruitment in schools than her advocacy group could. While her commitment to anti-militarism activity in schools continues, so does her union involvement. She is now a high-ranking officer in her union.

As with the service model, a social movement union may want to endorse candidates in elections or consider running its own. However, the union also defines its members' political self-interest broadly and encourages members to bring their social justice work to the union. A caveat here: Some members are going to object to the union devoting resources to "non-union" or "non-educational" issues. As I explain later in this chapter, there's an inevitable tension we have to acknowledge, but the solution is vibrant union democracy, and it is this characteristic that, for me, distinguishes the "social movement" union from one that endorses social justice. Any political position or cause the union endorses has to have majority support. In my opinion, it's better for advocates of a particular issue to lose a vote in a vigorous debate with lots of members present than it is for the measure to pass in a sparsely attended membership meeting or through a vote of the union's officers that is not well publicized to members.

Union democracy also addresses a thorny problem that reformers face when they are elected to office. How do you carry out your reform agenda and at the same time be an officer who represents the entire membership? How do you keep the union from splintering and at the same time be true to the ideals that made you become active in the union and run for office? The answer is that you ran on a program (I hope!) and it's your job to lead based on those proposals and ideas. Members have a right to know precisely what you are doing—and why. If officers, staff, or individual members object, listen and make sure that what you're doing is consistent with the program on which you ran. If it is, tell people who object that they have the right to take the matter to the body that is responsible for overseeing what you do. Make your case to that body and to the membership, and then abide by the democratic decisions that are made. In other words, be prepared to struggle as a leader to persuade the entire union about the ideas and values on which you ran for office. The fight for these ideas hasn't ended when you're elected. On the contrary, it's just begun!

Many teachers are fearful, understandably, given the weakened state of the unions and the ferocity of the attacks on teachers. They are demoralized and often believe that they are failing at their profession, and as a result many want to shut their classroom doors, meaning avoiding any contact with colleagues or thought of politics.[4] Many members balk at becoming more involved in the union because it seems—and often is—remote from their primary concerns. In the service model this stance is to be expected because members aren't supposed to take an interest in union affairs—and don't. In contrast, building a social movement union means encouraging members to use the union as a vehicle to take on concerns. Instead of waiting for "the union" to do something for them, members need to be educated that they *are* the union. They should be able to expect union support in organizing campaigns; at the same time, members are leading the campaigns.

The same conditions that are producing fear and withdrawal are also generating opportunities for discussions and organizing because school workers see that they need protections that have been lost or eroded. Teachers are asking, "Where is the union in this?" and a new generation of teachers is becoming politicized. They are offended, often angry, at tirades from politicians and the media about their ability, character, professional authority, and economic security. They are looking for leadership from their unions. Our challenge is to harness their energy. The challenge is enormous and our resources, financial and human, are limited. We need to be much more strategic in what we expect from members and to define our goals very carefully. In many districts the teachers union no longer has a presence at the school site, and changing this has to be paramount. The union needs a voice at the school site, which means educating members about social movement unionism and developing new leaders in the school. Though conventional (service model) wisdom is that the union's strength depends on the smarts of district or national staff and central headquarters, social movement unionists know that what counts most is the union's strength at the building level. Members need to experience their collective strength, the power to influence what occurs, in the place they spend their work lives.

Ideally this occurs as the union reaches out to parents, community, and labor, casting issues in terms of human rights and social justice, not just teachers' immediate self-interest. Goals are configured in light of how the school and school system operate. The union functions as connective tissue, linking struggles for a just, equitable society—and world—to teachers' concerns about schools and education. Struggles over cuts in programs should be cast in terms of harm being done to students, with parents, students, other unions, and the community encouraged and helped to formulate campaigns. In a workshop I recently led for union activists, an ESL teacher concerned about cuts to services that would lead to layoffs expressed hopelessness about altering the district policies. After some discussion she realized she had natural allies in parents of ESL students. She reformulated the issue as a social justice struggle, to mobilize parents and advocates for immigrant rights about the harm that was being done to kids with these cuts. She saw that she had to emphasize parents' lack of input and the current anti-immigrant sentiment that allows second-language learners to be marginalized. Though not expecting much from the union apparatus because of its atrophy, she also realized union members and parents should pressure the city union official in charge of bilingual programs to use the union's connections and clout to save the program.

We in the United States can find it hard to imagine a teachers union functioning in this way. Examining teachers unions elsewhere in the world that try to be social movement unions provides very important insights. While learning from these unions, we should realize they cannot provide us with a blueprint, a set of rules like a paint-by-numbers kit, that will produce the unions we need. Each country, each context differs, as do the challenges of a particular time or struggle. Even the best unions are a work in progress.[5] Still, there are important lessons for us. First, we need to acknowledge that public employees' credibility with the public has been damaged. Teachers unions cannot assume, as they did forty years ago, that most parents and citizens will be believe that "teachers want what children need," which was the slogan the AFT (American Federation of Teachers) used in fighting for better working conditions and salaries in the 1960s. We have to take a step back and build trust and support, perhaps as the municipal workers in Cali, Colombia, did, by volunteering their time to do repairs in poor neighborhoods that had been neglected. We may need international support, too, as did the Cali workers.[6] Second, we need to find ways to balance the demands made on the union for political work that is not immediately related to teaching and responsibilities to members. Social movement teachers unions need to remain labor unions, representing members, rather than morphing into all-purpose social movements. It's hard to imagine this happening in the United States because our labor movement is so far from being swept away by passion for social justice. But it's a danger that I think we need to keep in the back of our minds because this mistake was made by Solidarność, the organization of Polish labor unions, when they led the struggle to topple the Communist state.[7] Caught up in the political battle against the Communist regime, Solidarność ceased fighting for members' needs, as workers, on the job. The unions had to be rebuilt, in a slow, difficult process that continues today. While US unions and teachers face a situation that is far different from that which Polish workers and unions confronted under communism, advocates of social movement unionism are questioning the traditional union structure and collective bargaining responsibilities.[8] How do we reconcile our responsibilities to members' "bread and butter" needs with the unions' social commitments? I think the example of Solidarność is a reminder that there *has to be* a tension between these responsibilities. The third lesson is that when the union subordinates social justice goals to accommodate the agenda of its friends in government, the union discredits itself among its allies and sabotages development of authentic alliances with activists. Although public employee unions in South Africa were early, strong defenders of the fight against racism and apartheid through participation in the ANC (African National Congress), poor communities no longer provide the unions with automatic support. Researchers discovered that one public employee union's ability to build effective coalitions was significantly undercut by the national union's commitment to the ANC's adoption of neoliberal economic policies in governing, policies that the union's allies among community activists opposed.[9]

What these three lessons mean operationally for US teachers unions is that we need to keep sight of our work of representing members on "bread and butter" and working conditions; we have to develop ways of developing mutually respectful and supportive alliances with communities that have been ill-served by public education; and we have to rethink the union policy of putting its program on the back burner while we elect "friends of labor."

Social Movement Unions and "Bread and Butter"

Our opponents have been successful in eliminating or curtailing collective bargaining rights in several states. But even if the union has lost the right to negotiate a contract, it may have some substitute in "meet and confer" arrangements. In any case, the first issue is how the union sees its members' role in the process. In the service model, the union leadership may conduct a polling of members, but officials may already have in mind what they consider realistic demands—and an outcome that can be sold to the members. Negotiations are conducted in private. Perhaps occasional reports are given. These days reports are likely to state that little or no sub-stantive progress is being made. Often a contract expires while ne-gotiations drag on. Union officials complain, correctly so, that they can't get the administration to budge. Another scenario that is oc-curring more frequently is that the administration/school board come to negotiations with a long list of "givebacks" so signing a new contract means loss of hard-won gains.

In sharp contrast, in a social movement union, bargaining starts with the union leadership organizing ways to have members in each chapter/building discuss their vision of what they want and need in order to be teachers our students deserve. As Margaret Haley, organizer of the first teachers union in this country, ob-served a century ago, doing a good job in the classroom requires not having to worry about how to pay the bills or how you're going to live when you're too old to work.[10] The "wish list" from members goes to a bargaining committee representative of the entire mem-bership. Ideally, the committee is elected just for the purpose of bargaining. It works to create a package of demands that is then returned to the members for a vote. As negotiations develop, mem-bers are informed of what is happening. If the process is stalled, the negotiating committee asks for a show of support, petitions, demonstrations, creative activities. In my California local years ago, members brought sleeping bags for a "sleep in" outside school board headquarters to highlight problems with the paid negotiator's fre-quent absences. The "Occupy" movement is reminding us of strate-gies once used, successfully, and bringing new ways to protest that unions should welcome and adopt.

One essential change from what occurred in the 1960s and 1970s is that we must now reach out to allies to ask how they think the union might use its legal and political power, including the right to negotiate legal agreements, to improve schools. I can understand why some teachers might find this unsettling. After all, members' livelihoods and working conditions are at stake. Why should parents be consulted? Nonetheless, I think there are ways to persuade members that asking for input is not the same as having nonmembers vote on the demands or the contract. Final approval rests with the membership, and the membership alone. It's critical that teachers understand that we are in a greatly weakened position, and parents, students, and community activists are being courted quite seductively by our opponents. Add to that the unions' embrace of the business model and it's no surprise that unions are not able to muster the public support they need to push school boards to negotiate reasonable contracts.

In developing campaigns for contract negotiations, the union must frankly confront a tension that can arise between what children want and need and what is good for teachers as workers. In an ideal world, the union would never be put in the position of choosing between members' needs and the public good. Yet, because the union is almost never strong enough to determine the contours of struggles, and especially now when the unions and public education are under such sustained, brutal attack, very often union activists confront hard choices. It's critical for parents to feel that the union is not putting teachers' personal interests ahead of their children's well-being, and one way to do that is to formulate bargaining demands that take into account what we hear from the people we are serving. I'll put this advice quite strongly: It's suicidal for the union to go into negotiations with demands on salary and benefits and nothing about class size or other conditions that parents and communities see as essential to students' well-being. It may be that the union cannot win all its demands and must make hard choices, but to start off with a package of bargaining demands that omits parent and community concerns turns a blind eye to current realities. In states that still have laws that give teachers unions collective bargaining, the union will probably not be able to involve parents and community in the official bargaining process. Nor will the union be able to bargain for the deep changes needed to make education work for all kids, because of the scope of bargaining, as I explain in the next chapter and in my review of Steve Golin's book, reprinted in the second part of this book. These restrictions on collective bargaining make the union's creation of an unofficial process in which parents and community provide their input all the more urgent.

Getting Started

Because nobody can predict what's in store for teachers unions, I'm not going to lay out details for revitalizing or transforming your local. By the time you read this book your state may have taken away teachers' rights to bargain collectively. Or your school system may have been dissolved and your school sold to a for-profit corporation. In the next chapter I explain three principles to guide union work, but beyond that the way in which readers can help to create this new social movement of teachers depends on the school and district in which you work and the nature of your job. It may be that all that's required to become a union officer is to run for office. The individuals who hold office may well be overwhelmed and realize that they need help. Or it may be that the officers have formed a clique and are so politically and socially isolated from members, so used to exercising power by fiat, that any proposal for change is treated as a personal attack and sabotage of the union's well-being. Or in places in which lines between the union and community have hardened, it may be that what's needed is creating a new space for teachers and parents to discuss what's going on in the schools, bringing the union into this new space once it's been established. What's important to remember is that being active in the union or helping to create a new kind of teacher unionism is not necessarily the same as holding union office. You may want to start by organizing on an issue, district wide, perhaps working only with teachers or with teachers along with parents or social justice activists. That's fine, but keep in mind that for social movement unions, organizing has to be done at the school site too.

Social movement unions view conflicts with administration about members' rights and dignity being violated as an organizing tool. In chapter 5, "Teacher Unionism 101," I explain more about the technicalities of contracts, so here I'll only mention that each union chapter should have someone who encourages members to know their legal rights under the collective bargaining agreement if there is one, in state law, and in school and district regulations. In labor contracts this person is the grievance chair, but it's even better to have a grievance committee, so that more members are involved in contract enforcement. If there's a contract, the process may be formal and protects the contractual rights. In the service model, the grievance process is wholly legalistic. If a member brings a contract violation to the union's attention, a grievance officer, generally someone who has a paid position with the union, decides how it should be handled. Often grievance officers decide not to pursue a grievance because there seems not to be a strong case, especially if arbitration is involved. Grievances are complex because they are based on the contract as well as legal precedents about how language should be interpreted. This doesn't change because the union shifts its self-conception. But in a social movement union, the legal aspect of the grievance procedure is informed by a commitment to empower members to stand up for their rights. Pursuing members' rights on the job builds consciousness and solidarity and can take any of the forms effective organizing takes, perhaps informing colleagues about the problem or organizing a petition campaign. Even if a grievance is lost or a campaign does not produce a victory, the model of members standing up for their rights is educative, to members and to the administration.

Another challenge in organizing is that many teachers unions represent school employees who are not K–12 teachers in regular classrooms, like substitute teachers, adult school teachers, paraprofessionals, social workers, psychologists, and school secretaries. Almost always, K–12 classroom teachers are the dominant constituency in a teachers union. It's easy for teachers to overlook the fact that their union represents other groups. The smaller constituencies often feel that their needs and desires are not taken seriously. Social class or educational differences between the constituencies often exacerbate feelings that members who are not K–12 teachers are second-class citizens. A social movement teachers union differs from a business union in recognizing that tensions exist among its constituencies and being proactive in addressing them. We have a long way to go before the ideal of solidarity is the operating principle in any union, but that can't be an excuse for perpetuating the marginalization of smaller constituencies. Having a robust democratic culture in the union goes a long way toward making members of smaller constituencies feel that they are respected and valued. In a hierarchical union, classroom teachers may feel that their needs are being ignored—which they are. What they don't see is that no one's needs or desires count, except for the officers', and that the smaller constituencies have even less clout and voice.

Like all majorities, K–12 teachers can be insensitive and take their more advantaged position for granted. Even after many years of reminders from a dear friend who was a speech pathologist in the schools and union leader, I sometimes forget to include school workers other than teachers in my discussions of the union's challenges. Please be firm but patient with us/those K–12 teachers! We're educable, but it will take persistence.

Beyond the Local

I explain this in more depth in my article "Cracks in Shanker's Empire," which is included in this book, so here I'll briefly note some background that will help you understand how the national teachers unions affect what goes on in your local. In the United States, most teachers belong to a local affiliate of the NEA or the AFT. Both the NEA and AFT are national unions with state-level organizations. In general, teachers in the largest cities are in the AFT, which is affiliated with the AFL-CIO (American Federation of Labor–Congress of Industrial Organizations). The NEA often works with other unions but is not in the AFL-CIO. For over a century, the NEA was the main professional organization in education. It rejected collective bargaining for teachers, considering it unprofessional, and contained school administrators. However, in response to the AFT's agitation for collective bargaining rights, the NEA altered its stance and embraced collective bargaining in the late 1960s. The histories of the NEA and AFT are reflected in their organizational structures, which in turn influence how they operate. The AFT was from the start a labor union, and as with most unions, the main locus of authority is in the local. Its state organizations have little power within the national union. A portion of each member's dues, called a "per capita," is paid to the national and state organization. Most dues money is kept at home. Locals pay their officers if they wish and hire staff out of their budgets, though the national office will provide extra assistance on an "as granted basis." In the NEA, state organizations are the most powerful component. Dues are paid to the state organization, which sends organizers and staff back to the local.

The AFT and NEA are "business unions." We need to make them social movement unions, at the local, state, and national levels. The insider knowledge and cozy relationships union officials have with politicians cannot protect teachers' livelihoods and public education.

An International Vision

One new challenge we face is that the attacks on public education and teachers unions are part of a global project. Our resistance must be international, too. It's not enough for teachers in one community to organize or for a union to have a strong national presence. Education policies are borrowed and adapted through the international collaboration of the wealthy and powerful, in economic organizations and international summits. We have an important stake in the success of teachers' resistance elsewhere in the world because their movement helps weaken a common opponent. When Joel Klein, former head of the New York City school system, meets with Tony Blair, former prime minister of the United Kingdom, we can be sure they don't just exchange recommendations for good restaurants in their hometowns. In the next chapter I explore the challenge of international involvement in more depth, but any discussion about building stronger union locals has to mention how we go about developing awareness of the global aspect of this assault. We cannot duck this aspect, any more than we can address climate change by working in only one community, state, or nation. Neoliberalism's devastation of public education is a global epidemic that requires a global cure. International solidarity isn't charity. It's in our self-interest. We give help—and receive it.

4.

The New Landscape

Our movement has to work within a new political and economic landscape. Let's be clear that this terrain is not due to an act of nature. Nor is it inevitable, as our opponents say. Still, we should not underestimate the enormity of the challenge. Turning back these attacks requires that while we are fighting immediate attacks, we prepare for what's being planned.

We cannot predict all the details as they will unfold, but what we do know is that our enemies want to destroy teachers unions' institutional strength and legal rights. They aim to eliminate or erode the legal right for unions to speak on behalf of school workers. One way to do that is by eliminating collective bargaining through the legislative process. Another way is to dissolve school systems into loosely regulated networks of schools, as the Philadelphia school district announced it would do. This policy takes one step further the process of "outsourcing" public services and effectively "blows up" the system of public education created a century ago. Although we must, of course, resist these as best we can, I think we should assume that teachers unions will be forced to operate under different legal and structural conditions. *Every union should be preparing for this prospect now.* The unions need a detailed plan for collecting members' dues through credit card deductions or automatic payment from bank accounts. And let me be clear that a detailed plan means educating members about the reasons the union must be prepared. This relates to my point in the last chapter about what we want to expect from all our members—their understanding that we face a well-orchestrated project to destroy teaching as a profession and public oversight of schooling.

The union also needs to discuss, now, how it will respond to loss of collective bargaining or elimination of the right to bargain over health and pension benefits. To see what we need to do, we have to scrutinize and learn from our mistakes, in particular how the labor movement's embrace of business unionism configured our present crisis. It's not common knowledge, but several decades ago the most powerful industrial unions in the United States had internal debates about how labor should deal with members' need for health care and pensions. Advocates of business unionism argued the union should bargain for health care and pensions as part of the contract, making employers pay. Others argued for what I have called a social movement orientation, pointing out the need for the unions to use their considerable political clout to push for the government to establish health care and pensions for everyone. Most European unions adopted the social movement union approach and forced their governments to establish universal health care and retirement plans. Though these benefits are under attack in Europe as well, governments have met stiff resistance because everyone is affected by the cuts. In retrospect, the "practical" stance of business unionism was shortsighted, and it's a mistake we ought not repeat. Public employee unions have long defended our benefits with the argument that they set the bar for what everyone should have. Sorry to say, this line of reasoning rings very hollow to people who have no employer-sponsored health care or pension. The best way for teachers unions to win better health care and pensions for members is to lead the fight for single-payer health care and improved social security. In terms of practicality, the odds of our winning single-payer health care are actually better than they are of our getting improved health benefits in union contracts. Fighting for single-payer health care and improving social security is a win-win proposition for teachers (and other public employees). This struggle undermines the characterization of us as "selfish" and it also addresses one of the key ideas used to privatize public education: the idea that government has no responsibilities for the social good.

The hostile political environment, most unions' weakened organization at the building level, tenuous ties with parents and activists, and labor's diminished political power means we have to use the union's traditional weapons, job actions, very wisely. In the past, union leaders who had no intention of organizing a strike would "saber rattle," or bluster, about calling a strike without having any intention of carrying out the threat. Today saber rattling succeeds in frightening only one group, members who don't understand what will be involved. Without campaigns to win the support of parents and community organizations, a strike threat diminishes the union's credibility. I want to be clear in warning against saber rattling that we must be prepared to use the strike. It is our most powerful weapon. The British Columbia Teachers Federation (BCTF) is a fine example of how to organize for a successful strike, even when defying the courts. But the

BCTF has a history of mobilizing its members and social justice work that put it in a relatively strong position. Teachers unions that are rebuilding their strength should consider other options, especially a one-day work stoppage. This is a powerful and underutilized strategy that is a dress rehearsal for a strike in that it prepares members for what occurs in a strike, yet it is not open-ended. On the other side, the punishment the union receives may be the same as if there had been a full-blown strike, so the question is whether the union has prepared adequately for whatever job action it calls.

The commonsense advice here is that preparing for work stoppages of any duration means building deep support among members *and* the public. Teachers unions cannot "go it alone" and win. Given the enormous hostility toward public employees and teachers unions, it may make sense to plan a nontraditional job action, one that addresses educational rather than economic concerns. Consider the Cali, Colombia, workers who realized that they could not win economic struggles without rebuilding public support, especially in poor neighborhoods, where residents felt service had been unsatisfactory. The union sponsored a public service campaign that included asking members to volunteer their time to work in these underserved communities, making personal contact with community members. The union won deep community support in its subsequent struggle, forcing a repressive national government to back down. The Cali workers have something to teach us: We may have to rebuild support for public education, using new and creative strategies, before we undertake direct actions.[1] One strategy we might want to consider is to "occupy" the schools for a day, inviting parents and community to join teachers in liberating these spaces and demonstrating what real education looks like.

Beyond the Building and Local

We can't predict what organizational form teachers unions will have to take in response to policies that fragment school districts. What we do know is that our best defense against attacks to come is to restore union consciousness and build strength at the building level. That will mean organizing in charter schools, those run by the non-profits and the for-profits. Beyond that we'll need local and state organizations of teachers that are democratic, responsive, and activist. One source of support and information for activists in teachers unions is reformers in other labor unions. Labor Notes sponsors a conference where union reformers meet and exchange ideas, and for the past few years has hosted special meetings for teacher unionists.[2] New Labor Forum publishes material I've found helpful in understanding the bigger labor picture.[3] The Association for Union Democracy has invaluable material on its website about your rights as a union member.[4]

There's no escaping another challenge: reforming the national unions, both the AFT and NEA. Many of the problems we face in schools, starting with funding, have solutions that must come from Washington. States and local school districts cannot by themselves solve their economic woes. Even if we are successful in changing tax policies in the states, school funding will be inadequate. Schools need more financial support from the federal government, and leadership for this battle must come from the national unions. Another key problem is that both national unions have accepted the use of standardized test scores to evaluate and pay teachers in order, they say, to stay credible. The question is, credible with whom? Certainly not union activists, who see the unfairness in this policy. A former student of mine, now the president of the union at his charter school, shared with me his outrage and dismay about the principal's demand for pay increases linked to test scores. Thinking the state union would be of help, the local president called the union office, only to learn that the changes the principal wanted in teacher evaluation were official AFT policy!

In order to understand what's involved in reforming both unions, you need to know somewhat arcane information about their politics and organization. Bear with me, please, in this next section, as I explain this. The AFT and NEA are sorely in need of democratization, though they differ in their organizational problems and political inclinations. Though smaller than the NEA, the AFT is probably the more powerful politically because of its affiliation with organized labor and its leadership's long involvement in national politics, especially in regard to US foreign policy. Though the AFT national office operates within the law and is not tarnished by the kind of corruption that marred two of its largest locals, Miami-Dade and Washington, DC, the union president has virtually unchallenged control over policies and staff. Officers are elected at carefully orchestrated biannual conventions, which have little debate of substance unless an opposition grouping has organized well in advance to bring a matter to floor. The AFT national office provides perks to locals and individuals who do its bidding. Although I have not heard of an incident in which this has occurred, the national office encourages fear that locals who oppose the officers' vise-like grip on power may be denied services and help. AFT national officers derive their control of the national organization from their complete domination of the United Federation of Teachers (UFT), the New York City affiliate and the largest teachers union in the United States. They leverage the votes of the UFT to maintain power in the New York state union and use the state union as a base to control the national union. As long as the AFT national leadership can exploit its control of the UFT, and through it, the national union, education nationally—and internationally—will be harmed.

The NEA has quite a different culture and organizational structure. It has strict term limits for elected officers in both its national and state organizations. This means that offices change hands, in a way they do not in the AFT. However, this seemingly more democratic form of organization is offset by a different problem: While officers change, staff remain, and it is staff that controls the organization, not members. The NEA staff tends to be more progressive politically than the AFT leadership, and as a result, the NEA may take a more liberal stand on social and educational issues. The two unions do collaborate on legislation, but there's a great deal of competition and backstabbing. The AFT consciously seeks conservative (or neoliberal) approval by endorsing policies the NEA has rejected and then attacks the NEA for being out of touch. Consequently the NEA national office backs away from its more liberal stance. Voila! A consensus is formed—consisting of capitulation to our opponents.

Transforming the national unions is not going to happen overnight, but there are important ways to start the process. One is to improve communication and collaboration among activists within each state, whether they are in the AFT or the NEA. We cannot afford the luxury of having the two national unions compete for political clout or members, and the best way to change that dynamic is from the grass roots. Several years ago the AFT and NEA leadership came up with a plan for a merged organization. It was scuttled at the last minute by NEA members. Though their reasoning was partly conservative, not wanting affiliation with organized labor, the opposition to merger was also due to fear of domination by the AFT machine. I think their apprehension was well founded. The solution is unity from below rather than bureaucratic merger from above.

Beyond Our Borders

While we need unity among teachers in the United States, we also need to develop an understanding among US teachers that the attack on public education is global. We do not have the luxury of a "go it alone" approach any longer because our opponents operate internationally. We need information from unions elsewhere in the world about what we can expect and how they have dealt with similar attacks. We also need help from teachers unions elsewhere when we engage in struggles. And we need to figure out how to transform the international organization of teachers unions.

I realize that infusing international work into a union local's life is daunting. There's scarcely time to discuss all that's happening locally or in the school. How can we possibly bring an international dimension into the union's work, especially without alienating members who see the union's role much more narrowly? More than one union staffer or officer has asked me the equivalent of "How can I sell this idea of a global assault to my members in Iowa?" One useful strategy I've seen is that international work emerges from members' requests rather than from officers' initiatives. In looking for ways to make international aspects of union work meaningful to our members we're grappling with a problem that extends far beyond union activity, but finding links to global developments is a challenge we can't shirk. One connection that often reverberates with school workers is the situation of our immigrant students. Teachers unions can't equivocate in their defense of the rights of immigrant youth to a free, quality public education. This is essential for practical reasons (support from immigrant communities) as well as principles of social justice. Educating union members about why people leave their countries to seek employment here without work permits is part of the story we have to tell to explain the attack on public education. Transnational corporations want workers in every country to compete with one another in a race to the bottom—and make sure that schools don't plant contrary ideas in their heads.

Another way I've seen locals make international developments relevant is to point to teachers struggling elsewhere in the world with an issue that seems local, like use of long-term substitutes to replace giving teachers full-year contracts. Often there's a news item on Mary Compton's website that describes school workers in another country fighting on the same issue that's in the news in the United States.[5] For example, I learned that early childhood teachers in Newark, New Jersey, almost all women of color, were being laid off as permanent employees and rehired under temporary contracts just as I read on Mary's website that the same policy had been imposed on preschool teachers in Trinidad and Tobago. There was one important difference: Newark's preschool teachers weren't publicizing what occurred while teachers in Trinidad and Tobago, also women of color, had gathered parent support and organized public protests, gaining wide coverage in the local media. What if the two groups had connected and offered one another mutual support? That's exactly what occurred when members of the BCTF went on strike and their union was ruled in contempt of court for leading the walkout, facing huge fines. In response, the Trinational Coalition to Defend Public Education (USA) organized an international campaign of support.[6] Teachers from Mexico and the United States sent emails to the British Columbia government pointing out that the Canadian province was violating international labor standards by outlawing the strike. Although we in the United States tend to think our situation is unique, we have much to learn by staying informed about resistance elsewhere. Take the spirited, successful campaigns against charter schools in the United Kingdom, organized with the support of the National Union of Teachers.[7] Teachers in Mexico have developed a national coordinating committee to democratize their corrupt union, and the BCTF has much to teach us about working with unions in the rest of the hemisphere.[8]

The NEA and AFT belong to the Education International (EI), an international confederation of teachers unions, and use their money and political connections to dominate its politics and administrative office in Brussels. As I explain more fully elsewhere, activists in the United States need to understand that the NEA and AFT generally argue for policies that mirror the US government's foreign policy and shrink from mobilizations opposing the wishes of the US government and transnational corporations. This approach has caused internal friction because teachers unions in the global South face a life-and-death situation, literally. Teachers in Africa and Asia are resisting with great courage many of the same policies we face: replacing senior teachers with new recruits; reducing teachers' wages; and making teaching no more than test preparation. They are also contesting the AFT and NEA's grip on the EI, and in this struggle they will need our support.[9]

Summing It Up: Courage, Caring, Critique

As I've observed, the rules have changed. We're battling on terrain that is more treacherous. The extraordinary breadth and strength of the forces arrayed against us are stunning. What this new historical context means is that we can't rely on "past practice" or the people who tout it as a solution. To succeed, we need to learn from history but realize that the rules have changed, for our opponents and for us. I remember many occasions in my California local when we rejected advice from state and national officials—and admitted privately that we worried that we were risking our members' well-being in asking them to follow us. In retrospect, I can see that we were wise to have allowed space in our executive committee meetings to acknowledge our fears. However, we used our apprehensions to plan more effectively, rather than allowing them to become a fait accompli. Decisions based on fear assume powerlessness and limit possibilities. By all means, acknowledge the dangers—and then use this information to understand how to advance your vision. Having *courage* is essential to change the equation of what's possible. Keep this in mind, too: There's no use trying to go back or retreat to the familiar because neoliberalism has upended the social and political conditions on which the old status quo was predicated.

Often when I meet with union leaders committed to the ideals of social movement unionism, I see they are excited and a bit overwhelmed. Understandably so. They are trying to carry out their campaign pledges of making the union more assertive, and they tackle their new jobs with tremendous zeal and idealism. At the same time, they often feel their lack of experience in many facets of running the union's operations. In at least one case, just days after reformers were elected to lead the union, teachers faced unprecedented attacks from city, state, and national politicians. Worried that they weren't knowledgeable enough to deal with the state legislature, the officers followed the advice of state union officials, with disastrous results. Moral: You're writing the rules now. You need the courage to face that reality, head-on.

However, consider this: The ideal of social movement unionism relieves you from needing to know all the answers when you are elected to union office. Your job is to mobilize the membership and revitalize the union's organization so that *members* tell *officers* what to do. If there's a crisis, the place to turn for advice is the most representative body in the union. Your job as officers is to think through and research the options, which you present to your members, as your best shot at how to proceed. Trusting in democracy takes a leap of courage because we so rarely see it actualized. But once you've seen the tremendous energy and creativity released when a social movement takes off, you never forget its potential. Trusting in your members is practical because as leaders you often face people with far more power than you have as an individual. Your power resides in your membership. When union officials experience themselves as solely in control, they feel weak and act accordingly. They make decisions based on a stance of weakness and fear.

The other reason courage is essential is that we must try strategies that are unconventional and new for us. Some strategies we can borrow from the past, like the sit-in or factory occupation, were developed by protest movements. But while we need to learn from the past, at the same time, we need to develop different methods of reaching out to colleagues and building public awareness. While we have much to learn from history, we also have much to learn from our members. Take those "flash grade-ins" spreading across the United States. Teachers set up tables and chairs and grade papers in a public place, like a shopping mall, on a Saturday, with a sign explaining that they are just letting people know what they usually do on a Saturday. Public response has been wonderful, with lots of parents stopping to talk about testing or political attacks on teachers. Often teachers organize these events independently of the union. Our members need encouragement to develop more tactics like this.

Caring

"Caring" is not generally part of the vocabulary of teachers unions, but as I explained previously, winning the ideological struggle against neoliberalism requires that unions defend schooling's social purposes and teaching's nurturing aspects, a case well made by Nel Noddings.[10] Corporate executives and politicians cast education's only purpose as preparation for work. Teachers, in contrast, need to defend education's social and civic purposes. We should be forthright that as a union we want schools that are like communities, with mutual respect and trust, schools that support children's psychological and social development. We are educating the next generation of parents and citizens. Projecting this vision is both morally right and practical. The struggle to create schools that are caring makes teachers allies of parents in creating places in which we want to teach and children want to learn. Putting forward an ideal of a caring school reframes the debate about our working conditions, explaining our needs as workers and professionals in human terms.

Politicians have succeeded in casting teachers and our unions as uncaring. To undo this perception, unions will have to propose a tone and direction that some members, especially those who feel embittered or alienated, may not initially like. But I think a good union leadership will do its best to put forward this approach, especially if teachers in your district earn more money than many of the parents whose children attend the schools—and particularly if the district or politicians have used this disparity against the union. Here again, we should remember how Cali municipal workers rallied public support. The government succeeded in weakening the union's support in poorer sections of the city by using the kind of rhetoric about making services work for poor people that we hear used against teachers. The union fought back by showing its members cared about residents.

Although teaching as an occupation is mostly female, union officers and staff are often disproportionately drawn from the ranks of white, male high school teachers. High school teachers can care deeply about their students as people, but they often work in schools that are more anonymous and less personal than elementary schools. Also, elementary school teachers generally have more contact with parents than do teachers of older children. Because of these differences, when elementary school teachers become active in the union, they often bring ideas and a discourse that push the union toward the direction of "caring." Be sure the union dedicates time and energy to recruiting and educating teacher leaders in the elementary schools!

Critique

The popular media are doing a splendid job of educating people— to the worldview corporations and business elites want everyone to accept. We have to be on the lookout, constantly, for ways that our opponents' ideas seep into our beliefs. Often these ideas are not articulated though they underlie policies and laws. Space allows me to discuss only two pernicious and pervasive ideas that teachers unions have to challenge consistently.

The reforms of the last decade presume that schools should be operated like businesses, with students and parents as customers and funding dependent on performance. Teachers and their unions need to counter this with a vision for schools that are "owned" by citizens, parents, teachers, and students and funded (well and fairly) by the government. All stakeholders, parents, students, citizens, and teachers should be included in making decisions about what schools look like and how children are educated. John Dewey argued that we can't have a democratic society without schools that are themselves democratic. We need to make real Dewey's slogan, "Democracy in education. Education for democracy."

The other pervasive myth we must challenge is that we are stuck with existing economic arrangements, a setup that benefits the wealthy and powerful. We are being told we must accept diminished incomes and services, competition that pits communities and workers against one another, and budgets that cut taxes for the wealthy and corporations so that their money "trickles down." We need to stand up for a different vision and be uncompromising in promoting it— just as the right wing is in advancing its viewpoint. President Obama's rhetoric and his subsequent victory in the 2008 election based on people's (subsequently frustrated) hopes proved that this country has a popular majority that can be mobilized for principles of economic equality and social justice. We can build a movement that demands corporations and the wealthy pay their fair share of taxes, and that we as a society fund public services well enough so that we provide a safe, nurturing, academically challenging education for all children—and not at the expense of other needed services.

We are constantly subjected to the excuse that improvements are impossible because of economic woes. Here's the response social movement unions should give: The richest country in the world can afford to provide its people with good jobs and reliable social services—if it changes its political priorities and invests in people and life, not war and destruction. We should be demanding that school boards and politicians protect public education. If they won't do this, they should move over and let us take leadership. We saw in Wisconsin what can happen when teachers think big and are unafraid. We need more direct action.[11] At the same time, as we saw in the disastrous results of the NEA and AFT in Wisconsin pulling back from direct action to support an (unsuccessful) campaign to recall the governor, we can't rely on the national unions, electoral activity or on the Democrats or Republicans. We need direct action *and* electoral alternatives, parties and candidates we can rely on to develop policies based on our vision. President Obama's election and subsequent betrayal of the hopes placed on him demonstrates that the strategy of electing "friends of labor"— usually Democrats, though sometimes a Republican slips in—will not stop the juggernaut destroying our profession and our schools. The most persuasive argument used to support Democrats who could not be elected without the support of teachers unions but carry out anti-teacher, anti-student, and anti–public education policies is that they are the "lesser evil." Such was the case with President Obama, who combined his ringing rhetoric of change with the explicit campaign promise to establish more charter schools, continue with standardized testing mandates that his predecessor began, and to encourage merit pay for teachers. Still, the NEA and AFT endorsed him and poured resources into helping him win the election. They subordinated all other activity in the (vain) hope that Obama's election would end the attack. In fact, his administration's policies have been at least as brutal as those of President George W. Bush.

As I write this, we again face an election in which we must choose between candidates from two parties that share a commitment to policies that are hurting students, teachers, and our nation. The question of what we will do to prevent this from occurring in the next election is never asked or answered by those who say we must choose between the lesser evils. I think the time to organize electoral alternatives is . . . now. How that can best occur is a discussion that takes me well beyond this book's topic, but when a social movement union is working with parents and community activists, the ground has been laid for local campaigns for school board. At the very least we should seize these opportunities. They will provide us with valuable lessons about electoral politics. We are also obliged to protest the national unions' failure to help develop a real electoral alternative, so as to open up the discussion about what we need to do politically, to eliminate the tyranny of testing and privatization of schooling, to make schools democratic institutions that support democracy.

Critique requires that we examine our assumptions and actions, analyzing our mistakes as well as our victories, with a cool, objective eye. I think we need to anticipate that we will have missteps. What's important is learning from our errors. When this occurs, "caring" extends to our ranks as well, and if mistakes are made, it's best to make processes rather than individuals the focus of our scrutiny. This is something this new generation of activists is teaching my generation. It's easy to turn on one another when disagreements arise or mistakes are made. We need to remember that people are as important as ideas—and to treat one another accordingly.

The stakes are very great in our project of developing a different kind of teachers union movement, and the clock is ticking away. Our opponents are very powerful and they have a head start on us. However, we speak to deep human desires that cannot be so easily erased: of parents for their children's social and emotional well-being; of school workers for dignity and economic security; of citizens for schools that will educate the next generation. As we face challenges, we need to keep in mind that many of the laws and social norms we take for granted were achieved by social movements started by "fringe" groups not that long ago. In my college days, ecology was considered weird, even by radicals on campuses that experienced intense student activism against the war in Vietnam. Women earning equal pay for equal work was a demand thought too extreme by many students on the UC Berkeley campus in 1970. Gay marriage? Not even a dream of those of marching in the first Gay Pride celebration in San Francisco! New York City teachers electrified labor and education when they struck for collective bargaining in the early 1960s. Teachers forming unions? How dare they!

The expression "an idea whose time has come" is often used to explain social change. What this phrase obscures is that the time would not have come had it not been for ordinary people, like the readers of this book, who had a vision of a better world and worked steadfastly with others to make it real. Here's to your participation in creating a new movement of teachers committed to social justice and democratic teachers unions.

5.

Teacher Unionism 101

I am often asked by teachers and other school workers how to democratize and invigorate their unions. Where to start? There's no guidebook with technical information about unions, and besides, so many factors influence how you should begin to make changes. To help newcomers to teacher union activity, I define some terminology and suggest how to start this project. Then I share advice from Teachers Unite members in New York City who are organizing in their schools to make the union one that upholds principles of social movement unionism. Remember that the landscape is changing, as I write. Be prepared for new terms and conditions. In fact, be prepared to help define these new terms through struggle. That's what it means to have social movement teachers unions! Remember too that you'll be writing the rules, so take advice from union staff, experts (yes, me too), and other reformers as suggestions, not blueprints.

Getting started: In a very small district, you may want to run for local office right at the start. Maybe the leadership is just overwhelmed and will welcome new ideas and new energy. Great! Start with an office that does not require that you have specialized knowledge. In this way you can learn about how the union operates and make a contribution without feeling that you are taking on more than you can handle. In a larger district, you may want to start off by becoming active in your building/chapter—maybe chairing a committee or, if there's a need, running for chapter leader/building rep. Don't be intimidated by union officers' claims that they are experts and know best. They should be welcoming participation, not discouraging it. If there's animosity in the union between the leadership and reformers, investigate the issues to decide whose positions make more sense. Often forming a caucus will clarify the real differences in how the union should be run.

Collective bargaining: States give (and take away!) the right of public employees to elect an organization to represent them in contract negotiations with the employer. For teachers unions the employer is generally the school district. This process is called "collective bargaining."

The union's district-wide organization: Most teachers unions on the district level are affiliated with either the AFT or the NEA. The district union will also be affiliated with a statewide organization of the AFT or the NEA. Small- and medium-size unions often have an executive committee consisting of officers. They also have monthly membership meetings at which, in theory, policy is set. The largest unions have a representative system of governance. Each chapter/building elects delegates or representatives to an assembly or council, which, again in theory, oversees the union's governance.

The chapter or building: The union is composed of units in each school in the district. This is called a "chapter" or a "building organization." Union members in the chapter elect a "chapter leader" or "chapter chair" or "building representative" to head up the union on the school site. Each chapter/building should have regular meetings at times members can attend, with an agenda set by a vote of the members at the start of the meeting. The chapter/building should have a newsletter and committees that address the unique concerns at your school. Chapter 3 in this book has more information about building a strong chapter.

The bargaining unit: In K–12 teachers unions, the bargaining unit generally encompasses a particular school district. In some school districts the unit includes all or most school employees, including those who work in non-instructional roles. In other school districts only classroom teachers and school professionals are represented by the teachers union. After collective bargaining legislation passes, everyone who is designated as being part of the unit votes for one organization/union to represent the entire unit. Members can "decertify" the union, that is, choose another union to represent them, only at certain periods in the contract cycle. Since a charter school is legally like its own little school district, setting its own rules and policies, the teachers in a charter school are not generally represented by the union that represents teachers in the school district in which the charter school is located, and through which it receives its funding. Teachers and other school workers are usually not members of the union that represents other employees in the district. Nor are they covered by the contract, which is exactly what charter school proponents want: union-free schools.

The dissolution of a school district probably means that the bargaining unit is going to change, though a good union will contest the arrangements, so as to keep as many teachers and schools in the bargaining unit as possible. That gives teachers greater collective voice.

Grievances: The union contract allows for a process of making claims when the contract has been violated. This process is called the grievance procedure. The process generally begins with a member drawing attention to a contract violation. Often unions have at least one person who is a specialist in handling grievances. Members have the right to ask that a grievance be filed on their behalf, but in most unions members do not have the right to demand that the matter be pursued in court or in arbitration.

Union elections: Both national teachers unions are covered by federal legislation that mandates how union elections must be held.[1] The laws are quite specific and you should be well informed of your rights, which are considerable—but only if you know enough to exercise them. Everyone who runs for office is guaranteed the same treatment, and union officials cannot use union funds for their campaign. The election and the opportunity to run for office must be well publicized. And much, much more. One caveat: Though you have these rights on paper, enforcement pretty much depends on your ability to press your local leadership to follow the law. Still, often union leaders do not realize that they are violating the law, so know your rights. In voting, members assert their responsibility to set the union's direction. Elections are the forum for members to decide, collectively, what kind of union they want. They provide a key lesson in how a union should function, in its democratic commitments. Another consideration is that practically speaking, the more members who vote, the better the prospects for reformers. In most elections for union officers, a vote of 50 percent of the membership is high. A vote of one-third of the members is more typical.

When the vote goes above 50 percent, you're drawing in members who are newly mobilized—and in many instances, these are votes for change, votes for a different kind of union, which you represent. Then, after you're elected, the real work begins!

Dues check-off: In states that allow collective bargaining, many teachers unions have secured legislation to have members' dues deducted from their paychecks. In several places, teachers unions have lost this right and must find ways to have members pay monthly dues through automatic deductions from their checking accounts or have building representatives/chapter leaders collect the check each month.

Agency fee: In states that allow collective bargaining, unions have often secured legislation that allows them to collect a fee from everyone who is not a union member. The fee covers the cost to the union of negotiating and enforcing the contract and cannot include contributions to political campaigns. Everyone who benefits from the contract, that is, everyone in the unit who does not already pay union dues as a member, is legally bound to pay an agency fee.

Caucuses: A caucus is a combination support and advocacy group within the union. A union can have as many caucuses as there are members who share a viewpoint with others about how the union should operate or positions it should take. If you have an unmovable union leadership that's fighting change, it's probably wise to form a caucus with other members who share your concerns. You'll need to give yourselves a name and decide on your principles. Figure out how you will operate, including how others can join. The Association for Union Democracy (AUD) website has useful advice about how to form your caucus.[2] Labor Notes has a newsletter and conference that will put you in contact with other union reformers.[3]

"Nuts and Bolts" Advice

1. Stay informed, but don't put pressure on yourself to know everything! Get connected with resource networks and knowledgeable allies.

2. Know the contract if you have one. If you don't have a contract, your district has a manual of policies that it is obliged to follow. Especially in a work climate in which administrators think they make the law, you may find that school board and district policies support your position and not that of the principal or superintendent.

3. Union officers can be a resource for basic information. At the same time, remember their advice is shaped by their perspective. When they say something can't be done what they may mean is that they can't (or won't) do it.

4. Your aim is to empower your colleagues, not to have a single individual be the union by him/herself. Work to distribute leadership among all union members at the school site. Remember to include members who are not classroom teachers.

5. Try to have the chapter set up a leadership committee with representatives from each department and constituency.

6. If your school has an official committee that's supposed to be a consultative body, such as a "school leadership team," (this was a popular school reform in the 1990s and many districts still have them around, though their power has been sharply reduced), your chapter may be able to use it for organizing union members as well as parents.

7. Some union contracts require the administration to meet monthly with the union. Often this is interpreted as a private meeting between the chapter leader and the principal. While

it may be necessary for a chapter leader to have a brief consultation with a principal, this should not be the norm for raising issues. Instead, organize a consultation committee of union members with diverse views in your school to meet regularly with the principal to solve problems. Different consultation committee strategies you can try: Form the committee each month and find people depending on the issue; in advance, ask everyone to commit to one month of being on the committee; get the whole chapter involved in the consultation committee process. You might want to try asking for issues of concern at chapter meetings. If anyone wants to work on these issues, meet together before consultations with the principal, planning the agenda in advance, so that you present a unified front to the administration. Write up what happens as a result of the meeting and report to the chapter! This is essential to make sure to deal with suspicions or fears that deals are being cut. Another suggestion is to put an envelope or folder up in an accessible location where union members can drop off notes with concerns/issues for the consultation committee.

Foster communication among your school community—you should assume that the administration (or school employees who use the administration's lens in viewing what occurs) is sowing seeds of discord, suggesting that one group is being privileged at the other's expense. The chapter's best defense against this is lots of communication about what's occurring—from the union's point of view.

8. Organize a newsletter (online or paper—hard copies in mailboxes can be an important documentation/organizing tool) or listserv for your chapter.

9. Consider creating two listservs for union members. One shares official announcements; the other provides analytical/critical points of view. And having a listserv for parents is also probably wise.

10. Get your colleagues talking; provide a coffee space for chatting.

11. Set up a blog as a continuous resource with useful information.

12. Set up a weekly coffee with your principal if appropriate.

13. Find ways to support targeted union members as a chapter, rather than having their predicament remain hidden. Of course, the members who are being attacked must agree to this, but if they are asked about each strategy and the reasons the measures will aid their defense are explained, few people whose livelihoods are being threatened will refuse additional help. Coming together as a unit to support a colleague is a win-win. It makes supporters feel stronger and more confident that they'll be protected should they run into trouble, and it makes the member who's under attack feel less isolated and fearful. Plus, the collective response is often more successful in pushing back the attack.

14. Send mass emails to union officials, insisting that they take action to protect you or your school. Petitions are also a good organizing strategy because they provide a basis for talking with your colleagues (and parents, if they should be included). Members who won't consider coming to a meeting will gladly sign a petition, so it's also a way to involve more people in the chapter.

15. Defensive strategies—be a visible leader, cultivate allies, and protect yourselves. Speak up in meetings so that union members see that the principal's or administration's point of view is not the only one!

16. Emphasize to union members that they need to document interactions with administration about problems. They should keep notes of meetings and relevant memos, even those sent to the entire building.

17. Build relationships with parents.

18. Support untenured, new teachers through monthly chapter meetings and consultation committee meetings. The chapter may want to adopt an informal mentoring system, asking experienced teachers to inform new teachers of their rights and to help them with their responsibilities.

Part
Two

6.

Introduction

Articles I wrote for *New Politics* about teachers unions over the past thirty-five years are reprinted in this section, with only minor revisions, to provide background information about many of the issues I discuss in the first part of this book. Please note that the URLs given in the subsequent chapters are probably not active. Also, a few words of explanation are needed about what you will—and will not—find here.

First, a disclaimer: This collection does not constitute a history of the teacher union movement. Instead, please consider these analyses of particular issues or periods from my vantage point as an activist and researcher. In each article I examined what I considered—and still do—salient concerns for teachers and their unions, as explained to a general audience. The focus for each article came from events in the real world; my observations as an activist; and later, thoughts crystallized by my engagements as a researcher. All the articles are grounded in the political values and beliefs I shared with Julie and Phyllis Jacobson, the founding editors of *New Politics*, who first encouraged me to write for the journal. The articles focus on teacher unionism rather than education more generally. My ideas about teachers unions are grounded in my understanding of teaching and learning and the nature of teachers' work, but you'll find a full explanation of how I see the interconnections among unions, schooling, and our responsibilities as instructors in my book for first-year teachers and those considering teaching as a career, *Urban Teaching: The Essentials* (2003). Another caveat: Because I did not attempt to document for *New Politics* every significant event in education and teacher unionism, when taken together the articles have significant lacunae. The most significant omissions occurred as I shifted from being a K–12 teacher to a college professor and wrote about urban teaching and teachers unions for scholarly publications rather than *New Politics*.

Hence, one key element, my analysis of Albert Shanker's legacy, his personal and political domination of teacher unionism, and his influence on education politics for a half-century is missing from this collection.[1] Since this material frames the articles I summarize it briefly below (and retain only the most useful references).

Shanker's death in 1997 came after his having controlled the AFT for twenty-two years, a period that overlapped with his equally long tenure as president of the New York City teachers union, the UFT. The organizational structure and ideological commitments identified with his tenure in office continue to configure the AFT and its relations with the NEA. Contrary to the conventional wisdom, Shanker did not change his political worldview during his long career. Though he was identified as a militant in the popular press, from the start of his career as a union activist, Shanker was propelled by pressure from members to lead direct action. As an orator and political operative, he vastly outshone his rivals and opponents, save for a handful of radicals who had experience in the socialist movement, as did Shanker—more on that later. During the time in which Shanker controlled the UFT and the AFT, the unions grew exponentially. The UFT became the exclusive bargaining agent for more than sixty-five thousand New York City teachers and paraprofessionals, and the AFT doubled in size, to over nine hundred thousand members, for the most part representing teachers in large cities, who were more sympathetic than their counterparts in the suburbs and small towns to affiliation with organized labor. However, as I explain shortly, the union's growth was attributable to the political epoch more than to Shanker's savvy.

In a very short time after becoming president of the UFT and then the AFT, Shanker instituted changes to insulate his authority. One key mechanism was his creation of "disciplined" caucuses on the city, state, and national level. A caucus is independent of the union's official structure and can be formed by members in ways that suit their interest. Although other unions have caucuses as vehicles for officials to control the apparatus, Shanker borrowed a strategy that is more prevalent among left-wing sects than US labor unions. In "disciplined" caucuses, once the caucus adopts a position—which in the AFT was the policy that Shanker wanted—caucus members cannot express a divergent opinion or in any way differentiate their point of view from that of the caucus. Voting or speaking against a caucus position results in expulsion, which in the AFT and the UFT means loss of "perks" the union controls, like full- or part-time staff positions with the union. The political lives of union staff were— and are—closely monitored in the three unions controlled by the machines/caucuses Shanker created (the UFT, AFT, and NYSUT,

New York State United Teachers). This degree of ideological control over staff is highly unusual in other labor unions, including the NEA.

After reading "Cracks in Shanker's Empire" you will understand how Shanker's machine operated, and its efficiency and adeptness at dealing with challenges from the membership, including delegates attending the national conventions. Norms of democratic debate are upheld, but these are tossed out the window if needed, so that the leadership controls the motions that come to the floor. The leadership's other source of power is its control over the union's coffers and political contacts. These assets are used to bribe (with job offers or financial support for organizing) or intimidate (implied threat of losing support needed for a local struggle) elected officers of locals or state affiliates who are critical of the machine or the union's politics. As did Sandra Feldman, Shanker's heir, Randi Weingarten, Feldman's heir, uses these same techniques. As I note in "Teacher Unionism Reborn," the AFT joined with the NEA to suppress debate over a resolution about Palestinian rights at the Education International, using both bribery and fear of reprisal. No political opposition is too minor to be squelched.

During Shanker's rise, political life in this country was marked by the birth of social movements that challenged the status quo. The civil rights movement, then the women's movement and Hispanic activists, drew attention to social inequality, demanded an end to legally sanctioned discrimination, and called for equal educational opportunity. US schools and universities were shaken by student protests against the war in Vietnam. The teacher union movement was reborn in the twentieth century amid this intense political ferment that influenced the political culture of schools and teachers' self-conceptions.[2] Shanker's reputation as a militant, combative unionist was earned in the days when teacher unionism was a dynamic social movement nurtured by robust political challenges to the status quo. Many teacher unionists were active in antiwar and civil rights protests and saw union work as a natural complement to their other political activity. It was the movement that gave the teacher unionism its clout, not Shanker's shrewdness or courage as (liberal) conventional wisdom casts the history.[3]

Shortly after Shanker and the UFT emerged as important political players, they went head-to-head with civil rights activists over decentralization of the New York City Board of Education. Unable to racially integrate the New York City schools, parents and activists shifted their focus to controlling the schools in their neighborhoods. The sometimes violent confrontation between the white, mostly Jewish and Italian American, membership of the UFT and the black proponents of decentralization and community control intensified and mirrored a deteriorating liberal alliance.[4]

Shanker's embrace of testing and standards were long-standing, predating national calls for these policies in *A Nation at Risk*, the widely publicized 1983 report that called for "excellence" in the nation's schools so that we could compete economically in a new world economy. His conservative ideas about schooling made him a perfect partner for the political forces initiating the counteroffensive to the reforms—and rhetoric—of the 1960s and 1970s about equalizing educational opportunity. In "Democratizing the Schools," a *New Politics* article I wrote in 1987 (chapter 8 in this collection), I explain how Shanker became a darling of corporate chiefs and politicians pressing for policies that furthered the conservative backlash. (In retrospect, what we thought was a resurgence of conservatism was the start of the US iteration of the neoliberal project.) Shanker had for many years received accolades from neoconservatives, like Diane Ravitch, because as they did, he condemned calls for multicultural education, bilingual education, and mainstreaming of special education students. For Shanker these reforms were destructive diversions from "excellence" and were based on erroneous, unpatriotic claims that the nation's schools (and the society itself) had deep systemic problems with racism, anti-immigrant sentiment, and sexism.

Shanker's political worldview was formed early in his career. He and his most trusted lieutenants were members or followers of a tiny but highly influential clique of former socialists, organized into Social Democrats–USA (SD-USA). The intellectual mentor of this group, Max Shachtman, was well known in left-wing circles up until the mid-1950s as a socialist, a left-wing opponent of communism, and a supporter of the "Third Camp," a vision of social movements from below creating an alternative to both capitalism and communism. However, as the Cold War intensified, Shachtman jettisoned his anticapitalism and his former comrades. Since Shachtman believed communism had to be defeated and backed the US government in its attempts to do so, he assailed any criticism of the United States. Shachtman's views influenced the group of activists he mentored, including Shanker. Others in the group became high-ranking staff in the AFL-CIO, especially its foreign relations department. In an obituary describing Shachtman's two deaths, one moral, the other corporeal, a former comrade commented that in Shachtman's "turn to the right . . . Shachtman had become an apologist for American imperialism's filthy war in Vietnam, aligned himself with the ugliest elements in the unions, rationalized the racist practices of the construction unions."[5]

Echoing SD-USA's Cold War politics and its concern that labor not be too militant, lest it weaken communism's protagonist, liberal capitalism, the AFT aligned itself with the right wing of the labor movement in regard to foreign policy, supporting military incursions from Vietnam onward and suppression of labor unions that appeared to be too left-wing. As my report on the People's Summit of the Americas illustrates, little of significance has changed in the AFT's support for dictators, if they are dictators who are friendly to the US government. Unfortunately, what has changed in the past decade is that the NEA is no longer as willing to go head-to-head with the AFT on foreign policy.

Missing in Action

At least three topics are not given the attention they deserve in this collection. First, readers will find much less about the NEA than the AFT. One reason is that my personal experience in teachers unions, on which these pieces are based, is quite diverse but has been mainly in AFT locals. At the same time, much of what I say about the AFT holds for the NEA because for the past decade AFT and NEA locals have been fairly indistinguishable in terms of their atrophy and the acceptance of a "business union" model. From testing requirements of "No Child Left Behind" to merit pay, I can think of no issue on which the ostensibly more liberal NEA has held firm over time when facing the AFT's more conservative positions and attacks. At the same time, new currents are percolating in both unions. Still, the NEA's organizational culture differs from the AFT's in ways that are meaningful for building a new movement of teachers, and a limitation of these articles is that they do not address those differences sufficiently.

My intention has been for this book to address the articles' limitations in discussing racism and gender. Both of these relate, in turn, to parent involvement. As a teacher and union activist, I grappled with developing respectful relationships with parents and students of color, but when I wrote the earlier pieces for *New Politics* I was not yet able to integrate the topic in my analysis of teacher unionism. I think these omissions reflect a weakness of our organizing in the 1960s and 1970s. As I discuss in my review of *The Newark Teacher Strikes*, teacher unionism's incapacity to name racism in schools—and teaching—has had very destructive consequences. Not until I had worked with college students and faculty who were highly critical of teachers unions for defending the status quo and read—and thought—about the history and sociology of US education did I realize how essential it is to make discussion of race and ameliorating inequality in schooling central, precisely because acceptance of systemic racism has been part of the union's discourse and agenda.

A related problem in most of these articles is that while they articulate the need for improved schooling for all children, they do not deal with attitudes teachers bring and schools reinforce that are harmful to kids, especially in schools that serve children whose parents have little formal education. Here again, only after I shifted my role from classroom teacher to teacher educator could I formulate ideas consistent with my commitment to teachers' rights as workers and parents and students' rights to have teachers who hold themselves and are held to the norms we should expect of adults whose job it is to help all kids. This book applies ideas that I describe more comprehensively in my book advice to prospective and new teachers, *Urban Teaching: The Essentials*.

The first part of this book articulates the contours of relationships with parents that are only suggested in my *New Politics* articles. After reading feminist scholarship about teachers' work, I realized that relationships teachers have—or more often, do not have—with parents could not be separated from the ways schools are structured, which is inextricable from gender. The book draws on the idea of "caring," pointing out the need for unions to struggle to reorganize schools rather than accepting as inevitable structures that intensify the divisions between parents and teachers. I examine gender in urban school reform more in other articles, but it is a topic that is in great need of attention.[6] A network of teachers and researchers is supporting one another as we try to understand gender, neoliberalism, teachers' work, and teachers unions. Join us! To explore any of the educational topics I discuss in this book, you can look at my publications, described in my curriculum vita on the website I maintain in my capacity as a teacher educator. I keep teacher union activities and research on my personal website, www.loisweiner.org.

7.

"Cracks in Shanker's Empire"

First published in New Politics *11, no. 4 (old series) (December 1976): 51–57.*

While all of labor has been jolted by the economic roller coaster of the mid-70s perhaps no sector has suffered greater or more sustained convulsions than teacher unionism. The year 1974–75 ended with an average decline of 5 percent in teachers' real wages, and although they struck more and longer in 1975–76 than ever before in American history, teachers again saw their real wages decline, this time by 1 percent.

The economic retreat of the past two years is even greater than these statistics indicate, for they do not reveal the deterioration in fringe benefits that frequently accompanied—and sometimes financed—salary increases. In addition, national figures are somewhat deceptive because teacher salaries fluctuate enormously from state to state and district to district, due to the school systems' dependence on local property taxes. Generally, those teachers who have had collective bargaining rights for some time and those living in wealthier suburban districts have done best in protecting themselves.

Public education has never been funded ungrudgingly, but today the schools are experiencing a brutal financial assault that threatens their existence as a system. Many of the innovations and improvements of the 1960s have already been lost, and now the formerly "standard" programs, like art, music, and athletics are considered expendable. In most localities the percentage of school finance that is donated by the state government has declined in the last two years, a situation that has pressured local school boards to rely even more heavily on their local tax base, which is usually smaller and more economically homogeneous than that of a municipality. The declining birth rate has meant a fall in enrollment while plant costs, such as heat, paper, books, and equipment have doubled, even tripled, in three years.

Most teachers in this country are represented by the National Education Association (NEA), but the real leadership of the teacher movement comes from the considerably smaller American Federation of Teachers (AFT), an AFL-CIO affiliate. While the NEA functions in some ways as an independent union, it is still confined by its self-image as a professional organization that has interests independent of and even counterposed to those of organized labor. The extent to which the NEA has become more like a union, representing the class interests of teachers, by conducting strikes and excluding administrators from membership, is largely a result of the AFT's agitation and growth.

◆ ◆ ◆

At the helm of the AFT is Albert Shanker, president of the largest union local in the world, New York City's United Federation of Teachers (UFT), Local 2. Shanker is also vice president, in fact master, of the New York State United Teachers (NYSUT), until this year the merged organization of the NEA and AFT in the state. Finally, he is president of the national AFT and a member of the national AFL-CIO executive council.

While Shanker's base is his home local, the UFT, his reputation and power greatly exceed the number of people he immediately represents. His empire depends on his leadership of the UFT and his reputation as the founder of that union. New York City teachers were the first to strike and the first to win a contract; for years they had more influence in politics and organized labor than was imaginable for public employees elsewhere. Shanker, correctly or not, is given the credit for these accomplishments. For most union activists, Albert Shanker *is* the AFT, for he is the UFT.

However, both the UFT and Shanker have experienced a series of devastating routs in the past twenty-four months. The positions of about twenty thousand education employees, teachers, paraprofessionals, clerks, have been eliminated and several thousand more have been threatened for this term. Despite last autumn's five-day strike—for which teachers lost ten days' pay—UFT members still have no contract for *last year*; the cost-of-living adjustments promised by the Board of Education have not been seen yet and may never be. Perhaps the most humiliating and demoralizing blow came when Hugh Carey, the Democratic governor, who owed his primary victory and subsequent election to New York teachers more than any other single force, cut the school budget in excess of what the city's corporate overlords thought necessary.

All but Shanker's blindest supporters have been shaken by last year's events, but so successfully has Shanker entangled his own career with the union's future that the defeats of his leadership have made militants lose faith in the union itself, not just in the Shanker leadership.

Shanker's authority is much more solid at national conventions than it is on a local-by-local basis. All locals can elect delegates to the conventions, but more than a third of AFT's membership was not represented at Bal Harbour, Florida. Boston, Philadelphia, Detroit, Chicago, strategic Shanker strongholds, usually send their full delegate allotments. The UFT *always* does. As most votes are taken by voice or hand, the number of delegates voting for a policy, rather than their representative strength determines the outcome. For example, the last convention, August 16–20 in Bal Harbour, seated 2,262 delegates, 568 of whom were from Local 2, giving it about 25 percent of the convention body, although its membership is only 8 percent of the union. Shanker's convention strength was also enhanced by the absence of proportional representation in his home local. An opposition in the UFT will not be represented at all until its convention slate wins a majority of the vote; unless the winner-take-all system is overturned.

Shanker exercises his power through caucuses that he personally directs, in Local 2, in NYSUT, and nationally. The caucus is disciplined on the questions that the leadership considers vital. Caucus members may not speak or vote on the convention floor in opposition to caucus policy. Though many members do not feel obliged to observe caucus decisions in their votes, those who come from delegations that watch their participation must comply if they wish to retain caucus membership—and their position in the union. Local 2 is, of course, one such delegation.

Casual observation of the convention would have led one to believe that Shanker's throne was more secure than ever: with few exceptions committees rubber-stamped resolutions according to national executive council directions; floor discussion was desultory; Shanker himself ran unopposed this year and his slate included the last remaining oppositionist of any stature, Bill Simons, president of the Washington, DC, local.

The only delegates who were not members of Shanker's Progressive Caucus were those who had firm political commitments elsewhere. The Communist Party masqueraded as the United Action Caucus, roping in a half dozen independents. The Progressive Labor Party (PLP) did a persuasive job of making all opposition appear ridiculous by staging a rally, complete with bullhorns, in the lobby of the Americana Hotel; and during nominating speeches one PLP candidate topped that performance by exhorting the delegates on the need for armed insurrection against the bourgeoisie.

The convention saw only two sparks of broader opposition. One was a valiant though isolated effort by members of Local 189, the workers education local, to defeat measures that gave the Executive Council power to redefine a local's jurisdiction and by doing so, destroy it. Their fight was lost, but they won close to one quarter of the convention to their point of view, a heartening achievement given the convention's structural tilt toward Shanker.

The other notable confrontation was a pro-busing fight firmly managed by the Socialist Workers Party (SWP), which arrived with its literature and line already packaged, straight from its national campaign on the topic. Although busing is a critical social

issue that has a grave immediacy for teacher unionists, the SWP's
near total focus on that question allowed Shanker to avoid being
called to account for the union's drubbings practically everywhere.
While the SWP's emphasis on busing dovetailed quite neatly with
its own organizational perspectives, it did precious little to engage
the many delegates, including UFTers, who were disappointed
with Shanker but were afraid to confront their dissatisfaction, to
crystallize it even in their own minds. That was the task for oppositionists this year.

Busing had to be discussed, especially since the Boston local
has played such a shameful role in that city's integration turmoil;
but to aim most of the fire at Shanker's retreat on busing was to
toss away a good opportunity to demonstrate Shanker's inability to
protect the union's membership on vital economic questions.
Shanker's defeats in New York had stripped him—and the union—
of the myth of his invincibility. He was more vulnerable at this national convention than he had ever been, yet he was only once called
to account for the union's crisis. In her nominating speech, a United
Action Caucus candidate recited the calamities befalling the UFT.
As she added up the layoffs and enumerated the concessions
Shanker had negotiated, the convention became completely silent,
horrified, not by the personal attack on Shanker but by the enormity of union's rout.

◆ ◆ ◆

No union member who thinks about salary or teaching conditions
can reflect long without considering the AFT's political strategy.
A few years ago most locals negotiated with their boards relatively

confident that their district had the resources to grant at least modest improvements. What little impact they saw state and national politics having on their jobs was generally confined to curriculum matters. But as the financial strangulation of public education has been felt, teachers have been politicized rapidly. They quite literally cannot afford to be apolitical. Unless schools are given more state and federal aid, local negotiations can yield little more than trades of cost-of-living increases for jobs or fringe benefits for educational programs.

The pact Shanker negotiated in New York was but a more severe version of the agreements that AFT leaders around the country have felt compelled to accept, and just as Shanker in his own local refused to mobilize the union in a fight for more money, so in Bal Harbour he declined to organize for a national struggle to save public education. In New York the UFT membership forced him to organize the appearance of a fight, but he was able to escape doing even that at the convention.

Shanker mentioned the crisis in educational finance only in connection with the country's general economic troubles, with a warning that teachers' problems can't be isolated from the society's. He reprimanded the NEA for separating the attack on public education from the setbacks suffered by all working people, but Shanker joined the two situations only to whisk both away with an exhortation for increased COPE participation, and support to the AFL-CIO's legislative package and its drive to elect a president who won't veto it.

Shanker is, of course, correct in pointing to politics as the solution to the union and public education's devastation, but his political strategy can only lead to more defeats. Like the other AFL-CIO leaders, his plan is to hang on to sympathetic Democrats and occasional liberal Republicans until they turn on us, then defeat them. But Shanker, like Meany, has no method of predicting or insuring that the new crop will perform any better. Political action is reduced to political retaliation, a revolving door of promises and betrayals.

Shanker had to acknowledge the union's stunning political defeats in order to rouse the convention and the membership to shake off their demoralization. He cautioned AFTers not to have "illusions," that is, expectations of the candidates the union helps elect. In his words, delivered in his State of Union speech:

> There isn't anyone here who is not in politics who has not already been disappointed. You get disappointed. Yet get disappointed very quickly. The promises are great before election day. The delivery is very, very different. That is not an argument for staying out of politics. That is an argument to stay in there; for doing the best you can to make sure that the candidates deliver on their promises, and if they don't deliver enough, to make sure that they learn a lesson and are replaced by those who are able to deliver more of what they promise, and that is the kind of politics that we are going to engage in.

Two years ago, even last year, Shanker could point to several minor victories to defend his political course, but now his back is to the wall. He has been forced to make demands on the people whom teacher and labor's coffers have elected, and these politicians, primarily Democrats, have turned their backs on him and the union, in full view of his constituency.

Shanker is unable to defend the union consistently as long as he refuses to break from this political strategy for the corollary of his dependence on the existing political alternatives is his unwillingness to make the AFT the leadership of a broad social movement to challenge the method of school finance and the allocation of tax dollars.

He has no vision of organized labor as a dynamic force counterposing itself to America's corporate rulers as the defender of this country's poor and working millions. Instead, he views unions as a special interest group, defending their own members and sometimes other people, when their concerns happen to coincide.

Perhaps nowhere is the bankruptcy of this outlook exposed as sharply as in Shanker's inability to launch a dynamic campaign to win passage of the AFT's excellent legislative program, Educare. A comprehensive educational analogue to Medicare, Educare answers the problems of a declining birth rate and teacher unemployment by making the federal government responsible for extending full educational benefits, like early childhood projects and paid sabbaticals, to everyone, not just those who can afford these as private services. It is a sensible and sensitive answer to the union's problems and the aspirations of millions of people who want a better education for themselves and their children.

However, the Shanker leadership has done almost nothing to pass Educare, except to call a few press conferences and half-heartedly lobby Congress. Why has he not mobilized the AFT for national and local petitions and demonstrations, with parent groups, with civil rights organizations, with women's groups, with other unions, to agitate for this legislation that his own staff has developed?

Shanker supplied part of the answer himself at the very time last year he asked the national convention to approve the Educare proposals:

I have frequently been asked whether the Educare program is not in the self-interest of teachers and frequently those questions are meant as a kind of attack. . . . All unions are organized for the purpose of advancing the self-interest of the members in terms of their salaries and their working conditions and their job security. Now occasionally an opportunity arises when an organization can simultaneously pursue both the self-interest and the public interest. And those occasions are the happiest of times. . . . We should not be ashamed to say that we have the interests of our members at heart. But we should be proud to say that most of the time the interests of our members and the interests of the children we serve are not in conflict with each other but they are the very same interests and this program is a perfect example of that.

(Albert Shanker, AFT Convention Proceedings, July 12, 1975)

Here Shanker exhibits the same social myopia for which he regularly chastises the NEA. While the NEA isolates teachers from other working people, failing to comprehend that their class interests coincide, Shanker separates the concerns of organized labor from those of the rest of the society. His perspective recognizes fortunate convergences and unfortunate conflicts but can't explain them.

Shanker is incapable of leading a vigorous offensive for public education as long as he reduces the union and organized labor to a special interest group, for in doing so he shuns labor's social role as champion of those who need one. In viewing labor as just another lobby, albeit a big one, he accepts the ostensibly classless definition of the public that business and government expound, and he opens the door to the unions being pitted against the people they should be defending. Shanker's "us first" view of trade unionism isolates it from social movements and encourages its disastrous misalignment in the battles between those struggling to improve their lives and the corporate interests that desire to maintain the status quo. That perspective is damaging for any union, but is catastrophic for public employees.

Educare can be funded only through massive new tax monies or a reallocation of this country's spending from "defense" to social services. Shanker is unwilling to mobilize the AFT for the first alternative because he does not want to disrupt his political arrangements with the Democratic Party and the corporate powers that dominate it.

Shanker's ideological commitments deny the other method of funding Educare. He has been virtually unswerving in his support of American imperialism as shown, for example, in his hard-line support of the war in Vietnam and now in the AFT's enthusiastic participation in the AIFLD (American Institute for Free Labor Development). His views on international cooperation among trade unionists are an extension of his "us first" unionism, only in this case the "us" are American workers, not just teachers, whose fate he separates and even counterposes to the situation of working people in other countries. Just as he has no vision of the unionists in this society leading struggles for dignity and social justice, he also has no perspective of that occurring internationally. Finally, not only does his cooperation in the drive of American corporations for world hegemony cut off a most logical and mammoth source of money for the schools, military spending, it pits the union again those attempting to redirect this country's social priorities, people who should be our allies.

Teachers are paying a high price for these mistakes. While the new Democratic administration may well fund education more liberally than Ford has, Carter will not and cannot offer the vast sums needed to resolve the crisis. At next year's AFT convention oppositionists will have another chance to confront

Shanker with the bankruptcy of his leadership; but another year of defeats, this time under a government that AFT dollars helped to elect, may so demoralize union activists that Shanker once again retains his job while thousands more teachers join the vast army of the unemployed.

8.

"Democratizing the Schools"

First published in New Politics *1, no. 3 (Summer 1987).*

Since its inception, public education in this country has been viewed and used as an agent for social change, by the left and the right. Most Americans are like Mrs. Bloedorn of Brown Deer, Wisconsin, who, when interviewed by the *New York Times* last year about her political leanings, said she and her husband want little from the government except a decent elementary and secondary education for their children. "We built our lives around the idea of the American dream, that if you got educated and worked hard, you could get there," she explained.[1]

Mrs. Bloedorn's faith in the American dream, or more accurately, the mythology of liberal capitalism, explains why the schools receive so much attention. In this myth, schooling can overcome class, sex, and race barriers; every individual has the same chance of success, given equal educational opportunity to compensate for social inequalities. The Bloedorns are financially insecure and struggle, even on two incomes, to support their family of four, yet their attention is on education, not on the governmental policies that could provide them and their children with greater job security and higher wages.

Constitutionally, education is a responsibility of the states, not the federal government, and until Lyndon Johnson's War on Poverty in the sixties, Washington made only a small fiscal contribution to the nation's elementary and secondary schools and had a political influence to match its financial contribution. The War on Poverty was the Democratic Party's response to the civil rights movement's successes in illuminating inequality in the society, and its educational component was designed to provide disadvantaged students, primarily minority children in urban districts, with additional resources. The logic behind these programs was that educational deficiencies kept minority children from being equal competitors in the job market and that, given compensatory help in school, blacks too would take part in the American dream. The expectation that extra funding for ghetto schools would eliminate racial inequality was not wholly accepted by activists in the civil rights movement, but the compensatory funding was eagerly sought as a means to improve conditions in impoverished, neglected inner-city schools. Indeed the same problem remains for proponents of educational reform today who want to increase funding for public education without reinforcing the illusion that improved public education is the answer to class, racial, and sexual inequality.

It is this dream or fantasy, that we live in a country of unfettered opportunity for the well-educated, that prevented the Reagan and Carter administrations from cutting aid to education by even half as much as they wished; and although funding has been pared by 20 percent, the major federal programs for elementary and secondary education have remained intact because the liberal politicians who backed the wholesale gutting of transit and public housing subsidies retreated when the same was demanded for education. Conservatives, who deny the existence or effects of discrimination, are quite eager to eradicate any acknowledgment of inequality, but if liberals acquiesce in dismantling the school programs of the Johnson era, they will strip from themselves and American society the fig leaf of education's corrective powers, leaving themselves the naked defenders of the status quo.

Since state and local governments control education's purse strings, providing more than 80 or 90 percent of the funding, depending on the tax base of the district, they control what is taught and by whom, so education is resistant to national initiatives of the Left and Right on social issues as well as proposals to chop funding. The fundamentalists, to their consternation, have found that Reagan's presidency has been of little assistance in their crusade to legalize school prayer, eliminate sex education, and in general implant their ideology in the nation's schools. In each state and school district they must challenge bureaucracies that control the schools and are protective of their authority. Thus far the Right's most stunning national success has been in interjecting its rhetoric about schooling's role in imparting reverence for God, family, and nation in the debate on school reform. Now even liberals such as New York's Governor Cuomo, talk in these terms, substituting some ill-defined "moral sense" for the Right's advocacy of religion in the classroom as the panacea for crime and drug use. In doing so, they, like the

Right, ignore poverty, joblessness, and the hypocrisy engendered by unrestrained corporate venality as causes of the despair and alienation of the young.

When the social, as opposed to purely pedagogical, responsibilities of schooling in this country are considered, education's resistance to change is more understandable. The most recent wave of proposals to reform public education can only be understood in the context of a declining industrial base, shrinking job market, and increasing social stratification. What had fueled the discussion of America's failing system of public education is the consensus between liberals and conservatives alike that poor schooling is responsible for the country's industrial and moral decline, and any attempt to restore US political and economic hegemony must begin with the classroom. While the latest national reports vary greatly in their sensitivity to the process of learning, they are almost unanimous in calling for stricter graduation requirements as the method for achieving the excellence that rival capitalist nations, like Japan, have achieved. While the leaders of major corporations, like William Woodside, the president of the American Can Company, attribute their newly found and widely publicized commitment to public education to their concern about restoring the competitiveness of the economy and maintaining a pool of adequately skilled labor, their most urgent need is to use the schools to justify the gulf between rich and poor that has resulted from bipartisan economic policies. In the same year that American Can Company "adopted" a New York City high school with a dropout rate over 50 percent, giving it several thousand dollars in aid (a sum repaid many times in glowing press coverage of its largesse) Woodside assumed a prominent role in a civic coalition to increase support and funding for the city schools, and American Can proceeded with divestiture of its less profitable manufacturing operations, turning to securities and insurance for corporate development. If American Can follows the prevailing pattern, the relatively high-paid unionized jobs in manufacturing will be replaced by fewer positions, most of which are nonunion, low-paid white-collar jobs, and a handful of highly paid technical and professional slots. With fewer jobs to offer and greater competition for work of any kind, let alone those jobs that pay well, capitalism needs to explain why the "haves" have and the "have-nots" don't. Thus the focus on education has much more to do with inequality and industrial decline than it does with the quality of public schools.

The more conservative reports, beginning with *A Nation at Risk*, issued by the National Commission on Excellence in Education in 1983, attempt to restore the pure meritocratic structure of public education that existed before the Great Society programs were adopted to ameliorate social inequality, and the commentaries by conservatives and neoconservatives, like Diane Ravitch, Chester E. Finn, and Robert T. Fancher in *Against Mediocrity*, provide the ideological underpinning for the commissions dominated by corporate interests and leaders. These conservative critics attribute the sorry state of public education to the reforms of the sixties, which, they contend, relaxed rigorous curricula and threw standards out the window in the effort to equalize educational opportunity, which in turn was to equalize the society at large.[2]

The "back to basics" advocates in the mid- and late seventies were the first to challenge the pedagogical reforms of the sixties. They called for a return to the 3Rs as a solution to an educational system they characterized as suffocating in fluff, with courses in macramé (one favorite example of pundits) replacing acquisition of basic skills (which could never be agreed upon). This laid the groundwork for the current right-wing critics who build on the idea that the schools were seriously damaged by liberal reforms. Today's neoconservatives are careful to mask their elitist resolve with pious admonitions that low educational standards damage poor minority students even more than white middle-class youth, whose need for adequate skills is not desperate, as it is for blacks and Hispanics. However, the hidden agenda of these ostensible defenders of quality education for all is revealed by the glaring absence of program or policy suggestions for assisting poor minority students to succeed in meeting loose requirements, let alone the much more rigid ones they advocate.

One need only compare the conditions in any urban school system to those of its wealthy suburban neighbors to see how little urban schools, with dropout rates of at least 50 percent, actually help minority students to survive. Class size in suburban schools is generally 30 to 50 percent lower and support services offered by rich suburbs, such as psychologists and college counselors, are almost nonexistent in the schools of ravaged neighborhoods where the need is most acute. Without massive amounts of money to improve conditions in their schools, poor and working-class children cannot achieve any proficiency in the skills they need to survive economically or function as citizens. A menu for educational reform which does not acknowledge the need for a tremendous infusion of new money is an order to continue the system's present failure; if the menu contains increased graduation requirements without the new funding, it is a recipe for even higher dropout rates among inner city youth.

The conservatives compare contemporary public schooling with its complement of remedial classes to a golden age of high standards for all, an age which never existed, since the society has never before attempted to educate most of its population beyond junior high school. When the neoconservatives discuss educational reform, they juxtapose educational equality with educational excellence, arguing that we have lost excellence in the schools by using them to promote equality in the society. They propose an academic Darwinism to reinstate the standard of achievement we have supposedly lost. Ravitch, whose writing and viewpoint are aired frequently in the publications of the American Federation of Teachers (AFT), not only advocates reimposing the standards of the mythic golden age but also the same pedagogical practices, dispensing with the research of the last twenty years and the recommendations of the national professional associations of classroom teachers as well.[3]

In claiming a defense of "excellence," as Finn and Ravitch have done (they have formed the Education Excellence Network, a center for those committed to their view of school reform), the neoconservatives have given the veneer of respectability to the far Right's attack on the nature and content of schooling. They counterpose "excellence" to "equity" in the debate over school reform, demanding the victory of "excellence" in the form of more stringent traditional entry and exit requirements up and down the academic ladder to curtail the socially and intellectually democratizing effects of the sixties reforms. The Reagan administration's attack on the availability of loans for higher education and their terms of indebtedness goes hand in glove with William Bennett's recent attack on Harvard's liberalism. They are part of the campaign to restrict the acquisition of academic credentials while giving the Right an ideological hegemony it has not enjoyed since the fifties.

The liberal response, exemplified by the report compiled by Ernest Boyer, who headed education programs under Carter, acknowledges that special attention must be paid to remedy the disastrous truancy and dropout rates of youth. Boyer advocates more federal assistance to education, but the solutions proposed are only faint copies of Great Society programs that were in their boldest versions only minimally effective.[4] Moreover, the liberals fail to define "excellence" and lack any analysis of the reasons even middle-class school systems are unable to educate most students to think critically in any subject, a criticism voiced across the political spectrum, except by the fundamentalists and the far Right, for whom education is synonymous with the inculcation of religious and patriotic dogma. Even the most perceptive of the liberal reports, one from Theodore Sizer, which describes in sad detail the almost universal failure of secondary education to engage students' or teachers' imaginations, is unable to connect the crisis in the inner city school systems to the problems of suburban schools, which are financially better nourished but intellectually starved.[5] Finally, the liberal reports join the conservative in accepting racially segregated schools as a given; segregation's pernicious effects on white and minority students and the society go unchallenged.

The liberals never ask *whose* standards are being used to determine excellence, and this basic ideological flaw keeps them from cutting through the dilemma imposed by conservatives: choosing between excellence or equity. The crisis in education is at its core the same for prosperous and impoverished school systems: their isolation from democratic control and domination by political elites and bureaucracies, which reduce parents, students, and citizens to passive recipients of a service. Excellence and equity are not at odds with each other but are rather "irreducible conditions of each other," as the authors of the first, comprehensive radical contribution to the debate explain in *Choosing Equality*.[6] The report changes the framework of the debate on educational reform by arguing that neither excellence nor equity can be achieved without democracy and that the two goals have a symbiotic not an exclusionary relationship, contrary to what the conservatives claim.

Choosing Equality was written by several experienced activists in school reform and public policy and pinpoints democracy as the key to improving education. Its thesis is that the very same meritocratic practices which doom students in the inner city corrode education in the suburbs, and the solution is to empower all of the constituencies, allowing them to shape their schools as communal institutions to serve their particular needs.

How can a focus on "excellence" damage education? To meet demands for high test scores and mastery of specialized tasks, poor and middle-class school systems feel pressure to clamp down on students and teachers, making school environments intellectually and organizationally rigid, creating the sterile classrooms that Sizer describes so well. The middle-class schools produce students who excel on standardized tests but lack the skills and attitudes they need to be independent, critical thinkers. Students in these school systems can meet the stringent entry and exit requirements that inner city students generally cannot; but they share with the mass of dropouts an inability to live up to their responsibilities in a democracy, lacking both a sense of social commitment and an ability to express their individuality.

This condition, termed a "crisis of citizenship" in *Choosing Equality*, coexists in inner city schools with another, more destructive crisis: the failure to provide working-class and poor youth with the education they need to survive economically. The absence of democracy in the schools of minority communities, the disfranchisement of parents and citizens, has produced woefully neglected institutions isolated from the communities they ostensibly serve.

A refreshing strength of this critique is that it tries to critically examine the accomplishments and mistakes of the sixties reforms, noting, the neoconservative hysteria notwithstanding, programs were few in number and parsimoniously funded when the need is compared to the expenditure. Perhaps even more important, the authors reject the destructive error of New Left writers and activists who either ignored teachers and their burgeoning union movement or condemned them as inveterate enemies of progress. A close reading of the best-known books written in the sixties and seventies to expose the racism and authoritarianism of schools will turn up almost no positive references about the institutional role teachers or their newly organized unions might play. Indeed, the indifference and hostility of the sixties' reformers to teachers cut off the progressive critics from their most stable and potentially helpful allies. Fortunately, *Choosing Equality* breaks this pattern with its critical but humane analysis of the teacher's role in the school and education reform.

◆　◆　◆

Teachers are victimized, as their students are, by the absence of democracy in the schools, which robs them of the autonomy they need to respond creatively to their students' needs. Like other workers who organize, teachers formed unions because of their desire for higher salaries and improved benefits, as well as a thirst for dignity and control over their working conditions. Unfortunately, early in the development of teacher unionism, both the American Federation of Teachers (AFT) and the National Education Association (NEA) succumbed to a business union philosophy. They started advancing their members' immediate monetary interests at the cost of building a broad movement of parents and activists to wrest control of the schools from the forces responsible for the schools' failings but not accountable for them. The failure of the reform and union movements to address each other as allies robbed the radical activists of the institutional support they needed to survive and hastened the ascendancy of the business unionists and the bureaucratization of the teacher unions. As *Choosing Equality* notes, "Bureaucratic unionism has become the response to bureaucratic employer control" as business unionism has "not only increased the isolation of teachers from other school constituencies but has concentrated teachers' collective strength in the structures of the union bureaucracy and their contract functions."[7]

One example of the sad change of focus in teacher unionism is the public response of Albert Shanker, president of the AFT, to this year's "Writing Report Card" issued by the National Assessment of Educational Progress. The report concluded that most students can write at a minimal level but don't have the skills they need to communicate and think in an advanced society. Shanker dismissed the idea that reducing class size would improve writing instruction, contending that reducing the number of students the average high school teacher sees, from 150 to 80, would cost a great deal and compel the hiring of many new, incompetent teachers.[8] By sad comparison, twenty-five years ago Shanker and the AFT organized teachers nationally with the slogan "Teachers want what children need" and made reduction of class size one of the movement's key demands, to demonstrate to teachers and the public that their interests were identical and that unionization would benefit everyone affected by education.

Nowhere is the suicidal trajectory of narrow business unionism in education more obvious than in New York City, home of the largest teacher union local in the world, the United Federation of Teachers (UFT), New York's affiliate of the AFT. Its 1986 legislative report describes twenty-six union-endorsed bills that became state law. Only two may have any direct, perceptible impact on students; they mandate (but do not fund) direct guidance counselor services for every child in the New York City schools. Four of the laws will have some effect in improving instruction by requiring the employment of qualified home instruction teachers and teachers of English as a Second Language. But all the rest of the legislation improves pension and welfare benefits, making changes that are certainly justified but which only tangentially touch the crisis in the system—and the concerns of most of its teachers.

Isolated from progressive forces in the city and from other unions in both the public and private sector, the UFT leadership is unable to win even modest improvements in salary or working conditions for city teachers without appealing to the state legislature. Rather than building a working relationship with parent and community activists, the UFT bureaucracy tries to circumvent them and public opinion too, which it leaves to Mayor Koch to manipulate, and instead buys votes in Albany with its members' political action contributions. Thus political action for the UFT has become the method of *avoiding* a challenge to the political and educational status quo. In a similar fashion, the state teachers union, controlled by the UFT, in a year of intense public debate on education squandered its moral and political capital òn a law that gives each teacher in the state a one-shot "award" of $500 above the regular salary, only half of which will reach UFT members' pockets. The other half, a year after the money was set aside, still remains unallocated since Mayor Koch refuses to permit an across-the-board payment of the entire sum.

Spurning activism outside the union goes hand in hand with crushing it within the organization. As a matter of course union officials discourage any initiative from the membership and strictly control access to the union press, denying entry even through paid advertisements. The leadership of the ruling caucus routinely endorses political candidates without allowing for discussion of its selections in the union newspaper or even in the schools. The monthly sessions of the union's representative assembly are so obviously powerless to determine policy that only a small fraction of the schools bother sending delegates; meetings are frequently adjourned for lack of a quorum, with union staff (all appointed, all faithful members of the leadership's caucus) outnumbering bona fide representatives.[9]

The UFT's history illustrates that business unionism is a dead end, even in its own terms, but in reproving the NEA and AFT, the authors of *Choosing Equality* acknowledge the pressures that encourage teachers, as individuals and through their unions, to act in ways that are detrimental to themselves and their students. This awareness that the educational status quo victimizes *all* the constituencies to some degree contrasts sharply with the still pervasive tendency to blame teachers and their organizations for the damage done to children, a dominant theme of both progressive and conservative school critics. A recent book review by Herb Kohl, a prominent sixties reformer who continues to write about education, confirms that the attitude that impaired formation of a coalition between teachers and education's leftist critics two decades ago still poisons relations. In discussing two books by teachers who blame their students and working conditions for frustrating their desire to teach, Kohl scolds the profession and argues that "without looking at teachers and holding them accountable for their attitudes and practices we will never achieve decency in the schools."[10] He implicitly holds teachers *alone* responsible for education's deficiencies and improvement, and he puzzles how teachers can allow their schools and their unions to perpetuate conditions that destroy children. In fact, the real problem is that teachers, like most people, too often do not struggle to change conditions that damage themselves as well as their students, and in this respect they do not differ all that much from the "poor, hurt, damaged, angry people" they teach. By singling out teachers as the accountable component, Kohl inadvertently nurtures the business unionism that he abhors.

Kohl sees mainly that students are hurt; the union leadership focuses on teachers as victims. So the same book that Kohl castigates in his review is glowingly extolled in the teacher union press. Writing about *Out Last Term: A Teacher's Diary*, by Lucille Natkins, the union reviewer, himself a teacher, sees the "hopes, and all too often, the despair which unite teachers everywhere" and commends

Natkins and her colleagues everywhere for withstanding the "demoralizing impact of poor learning conditions." The article notes (correctly, I might add), that teachers will have little problem in "relating to the depression of Natkins's colleague who has to bring "wash and dries" to school each day because it took two weeks to get toilet paper for the teachers' bathroom."[11] Students are mentioned only once in this review, although we can assume that if the teachers' bathrooms lack toilet paper, probably the student bathrooms lack toilets that function, not an unusual situation in the New York City schools where Natkins taught. "Although their students do not always learn, professional teachers keep teaching," the review concludes.

Neither Kohl, the union reviewer, nor the authors themselves understand that teachers cannot teach and students cannot learn because a bureaucratic system frustrates the aspirations of *all* its constituencies, and it is the system, *not* the other constituencies, which must be held accountable and transformed. Kohl dampens the prospects for building a movement to improve the schools by singling out teachers for blame, rather than treating them as casualties as well, albeit ones who have far greater potential to alter the conditions which frustrate everyone. Individual teachers are no more or less responsible for the terrible harm done by the racism and class stratification of public schooling than are other American workers for the destructive policies of American corporations. Insofar as teachers do not pressure their unions to protect the interests of students, for instance by demanding smaller classes, they are shunning their moral and political responsibility, but they are also hurting themselves because they block the only avenue which can lead to an improvement in the quality of their work lives. When

progressive activists fail to challenge teachers to vigorously defend
their self-interest by rejecting business unionism, they also fail to
address teachers' legitimate aspirations and push them further in to
the embrace, really a stranglehold, of their union leadership.

Of the two national teachers unions, the NEA has come closer than
the AFT in recent years to addressing the need for progressive reform, but both organizations are ideologically entrapped by their
bureaucratic deformities. The NEA, which over the last two decades
has changed from a purely professional association to a union that
is an amalgam of autonomous state organizations, is staff controlled;
the elected leaders express the point of view of the national staff and
that of its state affiliates, an outlook which is liberal though lacking
even the limited class consciousness of secondary leadership in many
AFL-CIO unions. NEA locals are frequently just as bureaucratic
as AFT affiliates and the NEA membership, teaching in rural and
suburban schools, is probably more conservative than that of the
AFT, with a significant minority membership and organizational
base in urban areas. What accounts for the disparity of their national
pronouncements is their structure. The AFT, which was organized
by locals, has only skeletal state organization; whoever controls the
national apparatus therefore controls the national union. For the last
sixteen years Albert Shanker has controlled the staff, policies, and
publications of the national union, and thus they all reflect his now
neoconservative (but formerly liberal) thinking, tempered only by
the occasional concessions he must make to local reaction. Shanker,
with a far more consistent ideology, is frequently able to make the

larger NEA backtrack, marshaling conservative public opinion in his attempt to isolate his organizational and political rival.

The first major battle between the AFT and NEA in the recent debate on educational reform was on merit pay, which Shanker endorsed publicly, to the dismay of teacher union leaders everywhere who had long fought against such proposals in contract negotiations. By creating salary differentials based on performance standards which school officials determine, merit proposals enhance the power of administrators and diminish the teacher's autonomy, In giving administrators the authority to financially reward supporters of their policies with salary increases, and conversely punish dissent by withholding merit allowances, merit pay makes teachers quite literally pay for opposing administrative and systemic shortcomings that prevent student achievement. The NEA assumed the AFT's traditional opposition, and Shanker attacked his foe (the NEA, not the educational establishment) for refusing to yield to a new conservative tide of public opinion. He argued that the public was justified in demanding that teachers be held responsible for the job they did, especially given the understandable dissatisfaction with schools so grossly damaged by the sixties' reforms. The NEA leadership, sensing that Shanker had isolated himself from the ranks of his union, stayed firm in its denunciations of merit pay but never answered the issue of accountability. Almost unanimous opposition to Shanker's apostasy forced him to recant before union audiences throughout the country with the explanation that he had been misquoted and misunderstood.

Similarly, the NEA has criticized standardized tests as discriminatory, deleterious, and inaccurate, opposing their use. Shanker, who defends their limited use—which in practice the union virtually never limits—contends that the public deserves to have some measure of the schools their tax dollars pay for. The NEA has been unable to propose another strategy for evaluating education because the only other solution is one that transcends liberal tinkering and demands a transformation of our educational institutions: when parents participate in running schools along with teachers, when the schools are authentic community institutions, then the limitations of testing as an evaluative measure become apparent because all the parties can see that education involves far more than the mastery of the discrete skills measured in standardized tests.[12] Since the NEA lacks a commitment to democratize education, which is not surprising given its own bureaucratic structure, it cannot effectively counter Shanker's proposals and its opposition attenuates. This pattern prevailed in the dispute over teacher testing, which is the logical and equally misguided extension of testing students. The AFT has welcomed it: the NEA initially opposed it in all forms and later modified its position in several states.

The most important recent conflict between the NEA and AFT concerns the latest Carnegie Foundation Report, *A Nation Prepared: Teachers for the 21st Century*, which both Shanker and Mary Futrell, the NEA's current president, helped draft. Futrell, who signed the report with reservations, is reluctant to endorse the proposal for national certification of teachers, which Shanker has called a "revolutionary" idea whose time has come. Their differences are in part tactical since the NEA has far greater political clout on the state level where teacher licensing now occurs. However, the dispute also raises the issue of social control of education, now the domain of state and local government, for in advocating creation of a commission to set national standards for teacher licensing, the Carnegie plan attempts to create a national system of education through the back door of teacher certification. In determining who could become a teacher the national board would also be deciding to a great extent what would be taught. For example, if national standards required English teachers to complete course work in poetry but not linguistics, then schools of education would be much more likely to offer a class in the sonnet than in transformational grammar; and after being licensed to teach, the graduate of that school would probably be more comfortable teaching the subject he or she had learned, in this case, poetry rather than grammar.

Shanker welcomes national certification of teachers because state boards are "easily subject to political control."[13] He wants to see education "professionalized" like law and medicine, removing the political control that so often stands in the way of business union demands. In this "professionalization" proposal, which Shanker has defended many times in the union's publications and which was ratified by the last national convention, teachers are given control over admission to the profession and in return police it themselves. Parents are reduced to client status and political "interference" is thwarted by reducing the role of state government. The "professionalization" advocated by Shanker is the union's blind response to its defeats. As Shanker explained, "teachers are acting only in our own self-interest, wanting better salaries and smaller classes so our lives can be made easier. That image is standing in the way of our achieving professional status, for not only must we act on behalf of our clients, we must be perceived as acting that way."[14]

The national focus on education has raised the hopes of union members for improvement in their work lives. Shanker feels the pressure of union members for better salaries and more power to shape educational policy but is unwilling to organize the union's potential allies to challenge the status quo, so he has latched his and the union's wagon to the Carnegie Foundation's proposal, making the union, or rather the bureaucracy, the junior partner in corporate liberalism's attempt to regulate education nationally. The Carnegie report is in some ways an educational analogue to the now-forgotten proposals for a national "industrial policy," which liberals hoped would address the problem of the country's deteriorating industrial base by establishing a national consensus of corporate, political, and labor chiefs on economic policy; and it is doomed for the same reason that the "industrial policy" schemes failed to take hold: the old New Deal coalition is dead and won't be resurrected.

This plan to professionalize teaching is just what education and teachers don't need, for it posits empowerment of teachers at the expense of parent and community involvement; but its appeal to teachers is readily apparent. Many of the best teacher activists have been seduced by the desire for greater control over their own worklives and do not detect the underlying social and political design of the Carnegie proposal. They see the union's agitation for professionalization as a call to empower teachers and wrest authority from school bureaucracies and local political machines that are concerned above all with perpetuating their own power. The notion of giving teachers control over education also entices teachers who are wary of community involvement because they fear the anger and hostility of minority parents or organizations of conservative parents that want to eliminate sex education courses and pull books from the library shelf or, for many liberal teachers, both forces.

◆ ◆ ◆

The Carnegie Foundation, with AFT and NEA concurrence, has projected a plan which, in setting a standard for teacher licensing, implies that we need a single model for school reform, and in establishing a national commission to set standards excludes citizens from their right and responsibility to shape one of society's most critical institutions. Integrating the work of the best social historians of education with their own experiences, the authors of *Choosing Equality* conclude (I think correctly), that no single model of education can be selected because there is no one best system that will effectively serve every community.[15] They propose a coalition of community activists, teachers, parents, and students to develop school programs and policies that fit their specific needs. This can only be accomplished under the umbrella of a "progressive federalism" which would make the federal government responsible for equalizing school funding and protecting Constitutional rights, such as the prohibitions against racial and sexual discrimination and the separation of church and state. With this economic and political safeguard a coalition of the constituencies most affected by schooling would decide for themselves how best to use schools' resources, bringing the schools into the community and vice versa.

The authors draw on their own activist background in school reform over many years to suggest a few programs that have succeeded in bridging the gaps between school and community and teacher organizations and parents. However, the examples seem to be dim hopes when compared to the glare of past failure in forging the coalition that is needed to wrest power from the entrenched bureaucracies and political machines. New York City's war over decentralization in 1968, with its internecine warfare between the UFT and community groups, is a warning that the alliances, though vital, are painstaking to construct and easy to destroy. The fundamental problem is one that the left must confront in discussing *all* public policy and not just educational reform. How do we defend community involvement when the community is itself politically conservative? How can a progressive alliance be created when the allies are not themselves consistently (or alas, only infrequently) progressive?

Because Americans, like the Bloedorns previously mentioned, have such faith in schooling's restorative powers, they sometimes will become involved in a controversy about their children's schooling though they ignore other political activities, even voting. The mythology that education has the ability to restore the society to sound health further contributes to making education an important public concern; but as vital as it is for progressives to join the debate on educational reform and work with parents and community groups in trying to improve the schools, it is equally important to point out that education neither creates economic and race divisions nor can it by itself erase them. A progressive movement for school reform should be cautious not to attempt to be more than the educational wing of a broader movement to transform American society. Even successful schools will not make minority youths employable when there are not enough jobs and racial discrimination persists. Schools should not be held responsible for the results of national economic policy.

What activists can accomplish now is to involve parents, teachers, and a range of community groups in activity on issues of mutual importance, even matters that seem to have no broad political implications. The personal contacts that are made in a struggle about funding for an after-school program may be used later in a conflict over bilingual classes. Even when the conservatism of one of the parties impedes cooperation on a particular problem, the door should be left open for cooperation on other issues. For example, the joint struggle of teacher, parent, and community organizations against closing a neighborhood school can create links that will weather disagreement over a more divisive issue like student rights. What is far more important than consensus on any given problem is the mutual understanding that all of the constituencies are wedded to each other because of their self-interest and that none can advance at the expense of the other.

Most Americans have more immediate, sustained contact with the schools than they do any other governmental institution, unless they are incarcerated. Schools generally have some neighborhood ties, even those in monolithic urban systems and communities that are so fragmented that they are barely identifiable as being communities. These two factors together can make educational reform a classroom for the Left to learn how to build a popular, democratic movement that can help challenge the premises of American capitalism, as well as improve the lives of millions of teachers and children.

9.

"Class, Gender, and Race in the Newark Teacher Strikes"

First published as a review of The Newark Teacher Strikes: Hopes on the Line *by Steve Golin (Rutgers University Press, 2002) in* New Politics *9, no. 2 (new series) (Winter 2003).*

Drawing on primary and secondary sources as well as extensive oral interviews with participants in the events, Steve Golin's fine book describes the formation of the Newark Teachers Union and its heart-breaking confrontation with black nationalism and African American parents. He tells an engrossing story that is simultaneously respectful to the activists whose struggle he documents, supportive of their aspirations to be treated with dignity as workers, and critical of the ideological limitations that led to the violent strike and battle with black parents. This story of the Newark teachers crosses boundaries of many fields of history. As Golin correctly comments, it is "urban history as the history of education, it is labor history brought up to date as the unionization of public sector

workers, and it is a study of ethnicity, gender, and race in class formation" as well as "a book about the 1960s, one of a growing number of local studies" (p. 6). Although I am not a historian and cannot
evaluate the book as a historian might, I can advise readers of *New
Politics* who are interested in education, unions, gender politics, race,
and social justice to put Golin's book high on their reading lists.

The Newark Teacher Strikes is a narrative about teachers who
built the union and led it through two strikes, facing mass arrest,
jail, and loss of their jobs. The story begins with an insightful analysis of the motivations of people like Hannah Litzky and Bob
Lowenstein, who started the union, Local 481, in 1937. Most of
the union's founders were Jewish high school teachers from families
with radical and socialist leanings who saw the struggle for teacher
unionism as a vehicle for advancing social justice. These pioneers
were joined in the 1960s by a group of Italian American activists,
like Tony Ficcio, who pushed the union to focus on collective bargaining and more immediate economic concerns of teachers. Two
of the Italian American male activists were elementary school
teachers who expressed resentment felt by elementary teachers toward teachers in higher grades: "The lower you go in school, the
harder you work" (p. 18).

Golin notes that activists were aware of a tension between "the
new strand of bread-and-butter unionism and the older strand of
socially committed unionism" (p. 29), and comments that not all the
teachers active in the union during this time experienced the conflict
in the ethnic terms he has used in the book to configure the difference. Typical of the way Golin allows the voices of Newark teachers
whom he interviewed to come through in this narrative is his description of two teachers' critique of his analysis: "Doesn't ethnicity

hide class? Weren't Jews really more middle class, and Italians more working class?" (p. 29). Golin's response is that the Italians and Jews made different sense of their working-class identity. Italian teachers tended to define class "in terms of relations on the job: employees versus management. Jewish teachers were more likely to define the working class politically, in terms of what it had already accomplished in transforming American society and might yet accomplish" (p. 29). Golin concludes that ethnicity and class identity mutually reinforced each other and influenced but did not determine how individuals might regard themselves and the issues the union confronted.

Golin looks at race as well, explaining that although the union "aggressively courted African American teachers" (p. 30) during the collective bargaining campaigns in the 1960s, seeking to sign up teachers like Janice Adams, a Newark native who eventually joined and became an activist, black teachers rarely signed up immediately. Because of their exclusion from many unions, few African American teachers grew up with the pro-union sentiments Italian and Jewish teachers brought to teaching, along with a proclivity to join the union in its early years, before collective bargaining was possible. When black teachers did join, their explanation and reasoning related to the history of slavery, or as teacher Charles Nolley said when told to remain after school to work with no pay, "That's bondage" (p. 31).

Golin does a strong job of explaining how gender, especially a sense of what it meant to be a man, influenced the way teachers understood their identity as teachers and unionists. For instance, he observes that when Bob Lowenstein talked about his dignity as a worker, he "spoke from a long tradition of masculine independence."

Also, he observes that the organizing in the '60s was done by men who were not especially sensitive to the nuances of gender" (p. 20), a point not often understood by historians. Though Golin is alert to gender as an influence on identity formation he misses the gendered aspects of the tension between elementary and high school teachers, perhaps because in Newark two male elementary school teachers were leaders of the union. Another reason the book misses the gendered division between elementary and high school teachers is a factor I return to later in the review, the ways in which the definition of work is itself a gendered construct.

In the first strike, a three-week stoppage in 1970, black and white teachers fought for the union to have a say in decision-making. Golin traces the evolution of the demands, demonstrating that the monetary demands were part of a social movement to make teachers' voices heard in decisions about their work. In the second, eleven-week strike in 1971 that erupted over a union provision to eliminate "nonprofessional" duties as well as the board's attempt to revoke binding arbitration, many black teachers crossed the lines, siding with the board and parents. The strikes led to mass arrests and eventually to teachers serving jail terms of up to three months, also described in the book. The second strike became violent and polarized Newark racially, pitting the union and its supporters, among them Anthony Imperiale and his Italian American white supremacists, against black activists and the black mayor, Kenneth Gibson.

The story of the second strike is one that continues today, a destructive conflict between two forces that should and could be allies: teacher unions battling for better wages and a voice for city teachers in school policy are pitted (and pit themselves) against poor, minority parents and activists organizing to improve schools that have failed to educate children. In Newark the alliance was undercut because "the protagonists denied each other's legitimacy" (p. 112). Golin is careful to show that the denial on the part of both sides in Newark was mutual and symbiotic. "Striking teachers saw their struggle as one of working people against management. Their opponents saw Black parents and citizens against white teachers. There was tremendous pressure to choose between these two competing views, rather than to seek what was true in each. . . . Either the strike was seen through the lens of class, or it was seen through the lens of race" (p. 140).

Black teachers were under the most pressure and ultimately many who were union members identified "community" with race and crossed picket lines. Even when the strike ended the strife did not, and many striking teachers returned to schools at which parents physically barred them from entering. Golin notes, correctly I think, that an alternative possibility was for a teacher-parent alliance, which occurred in a few schools, ones in which teachers had been proactive in reaching across the border of race and class—and as I will explain, gender—to parents.

Defining "Work"

The full explanation of why the union failed to reach out to parents, to regard them as partners and allies, includes not only the issues Golin analyzes, but also one he misses, the way that teaching as work is affected by a definition of "work" that is gendered. As Sari Biklen explains in her book *Schoolwork*, "work" is defined in traditional sociology as what we do outside the home, so "family" or "home" and "work" or "career" are opposites. If one accepts this dichotomy as natural, immutable, or given, what should we make of paid labor, "work," done outside the home that consists of functions mothers traditionally do in the home, like caring for children? Taking into account the gendered construct of work explains the perception of teaching as "women's work" and other things that are germane to Golin's analysis. For instance, why teaching has low status and why it is not well paid or well regarded in the dominant society—or considered "work" at all by many academics whom one might expect to be interested in the subject of teacher unions and teaching, including labor historians, feminists, and educational researchers. A full explanation of why teaching and teachers have been unpalatable topics for leftist academics in the United States is not possible in this review, but a brief examination is important to understand why the gendered construction of work and teaching is central to teaching's low status in the society and the academy.

First we should understand the circumstances that make the absence of attention to teachers noteworthy. Overall, more than two-thirds of all teachers are female, and as students' ages rise, the proportion of female teachers in the school declines steeply. Public school teaching is one of the largest occupational groups in the nation, with more than two million workers organized into unions in almost every community. Even in states that do not have automatic dues payment or mandatory union fees, social norms within schools prompt a majority of teachers to join their local affiliate of the National Education Association or American Federation of Teachers. (The exception is in states that have not yet legalized collective bargaining for teacher public employees.)

Despite the size of these organizations and their predominantly female membership, teacher unionism was not taken up by academics interested in labor, women's rights, or educational reform until the late '70s, when *History of Education* carried an article about Margaret Haley, a socialist elementary teacher in Chicago who organized the first local of the American Federation of Teachers. *Labor History* carried an article (and cover photo) about women miners almost a decade before it mentioned teacher unionism, in an interview with Dave Selden, the one-time president of the American Federation of Teachers who was ousted by Albert Shanker. Certainly the romanticization of the "real" working class, the industrial proletariat, is a factor that partly explains the lack of interest in teachers, despite the fact that during the '60s and early '70s almost every major city in the United States saw the emergence of militant teacher unions, as Newark did. I argue, however, that one cannot fully understand the construction of the "real" working class without acknowledging the gendered construction of work that makes some occupations "real work" and the workers the "real working class."

For feminist academics writing in *Signs*, examining challenges faced by female professionals, like school administrators, was of much more interest than scrutinizing teachers or their unions. Their disinclination to examine the subject of teaching as work, an occupation that has been identified as "women's true profession" since the Civil War, was probably nurtured by the anti-working-class bias that was prevalent in the New Left and the student movement, the breeding ground for the women's liberation movement, or second-wave feminism as it is now called. And as feminism became lodged in the university, the class stratification of higher education certainly made intellectual work about teachers, who are primarily working class and lower middle class in their social class origins, less inviting.

Even now among educational researchers there is not much interest in teachers' work and teacher unionism. Although the American Educational Research Association, the professional organization to which most educational researchers belong, has a small "special interest group" for researchers interested in teachers' work and teacher unionism, a majority of its members reside outside the United States. Although they maintain research departments, neither the NEA nor the AFT has much interest in the scholarly examination of class or gender issues in teaching, nor of teacher unionism itself. Their lack of concern mirrors the stance of much of organized labor in the United States.

The Gendered Construction of Work

One explanation for the absence of much intellectually serious study of teachers' work in the United States is the class bias embedded in and supported by our stratified system of higher education, coupled with the ideological blinders that have traditionally kept class as an object of study off the radar screen of academics and unions. However, the gendered construction of work and teaching's low status due to this construction is a factor as well, seen simultaneously in the research university's notorious disregard for the quality of instruction in its own classrooms and in the lack of resources devoted to teaching and education as subjects and objects of study. A little known fact about university finances is that because of the practice of having students do practice teaching in schools while paying hefty tuition to the university, teacher education is a "cash cow" for higher education. Yet the money that teacher education brings in is almost never returned to its source. Teacher education's low status even within schools of education themselves is demonstrated by another phenomenon that is rarely acknowledged: The closer faculty members' work takes them to schools and young children, the lower their salaries, the higher their teaching loads, and the greater the proportion of females and minorities.

The Newark Teacher Strikes demonstrates not only that teaching and teacher unionism provide rich territory that should be mined for insights about the formation of class consciousness but also that one cannot make sense of what occurs in teaching or schools or teacher unions without reference to gender. One of the arguments that has bedeviled teacher unionism is how to deal with the issue of professionalism. If we want to elevate the regard in which teaching is held because we think it is socially useful work that is difficult and deserving of recognition and remuneration, how should we proceed? Should we try to make teaching like the other professions that have high status, such as law and medicine? Or should we propose that teachers act like other workers who want to improve their income by forming a union? But is teaching a working-class occupation? In his rumination about "Who is working class?" (p. 23) Golin writes: "Of course teachers are working class. Of course they are not working class. That's what it means to be working class: to be defined by your role as worker, and to struggle to be more than your role" (p. 24).

Understanding that the "role" of teacher is gendered allows us to understand in a different way the reluctance of elementary school teachers to join the union and their identification with a sense of "professional obligation to serve students," as was true of Edith Counts, an African American teacher who did not join the union. Golin's account makes clear that the Newark Teachers Union defined "professionalism" in a way that did not encourage teachers, especially elementary school teachers, who understood their work as serving children and families, not a school system or an institution, to join—unless they agreed that the well being of the particular children they were dedicated to serve could not be advanced without a commitment to social progress and social justice generally. Or as Vic Cascella described this definition of being professional, "you had to be concerned with civil rights, you had to be concerned with the learning of the kids" (p. 23). I explain below why one reason that race and class became constructed in opposition to one another in the second strike was that the union never allowed for a definition of professionalism that took into account the gendered nature of teachers' work, the importance of teaching's "mothering" functions.

As Golin demonstrates, teachers' notions about their relations with parents, children, and the subjects they teach influence not only how they teach but also their conception of what a union should be. Teachers who consider themselves in service to communities often view the school as an extension of the family in socializing and educating children. Because of this definition of their work, they are more likely to experience the tensions that emerge from unionization.

Successful teaching (like parenting) demands attention to children's needs, which are individual, personal, and at times seem to have no limit. Especially in cities, teachers work with children in schools that are hierarchical and bureaucratic, impersonal and anonymous. Teachers are treated as expendable and interchangeable, while to do their jobs well they must take moral responsibility for children's well being. So to represent teachers' interests, a union must take up the conditions that make teaching a job like any other.

Albert Shanker, long-time boss of the American Federation of Teachers and the New York affiliate, articulated clearly and well this function of a teachers union. But what his vision of teaching and unionism excluded was acknowledgment of the inevitable contradictions that arise between teachers' personal and individual responsibility for children, the ways their work continues the functions of the family, and the location of these functions in a bureaucracy as paid labor. While this contradiction is exacerbated by conditions of scarce resources it is not eliminated entirely even when financial support for schools is ample.

This tension emerges as a conflict in decisions about how non-classroom duties such as supervising children at lunch or on the playground should be handled. Most teachers loathe these duties because they are so far removed from intellectual aspects of teaching, the responsibilities that make teaching seem more than "babysitting"—or understood in terms of work's gendered construction, more like "work" and less like "home." However, if we view schools as extensions of the family and home, then another way to view these responsibilities is that they represent the school's role in children's socialization, so functions like supervising children at play are no less essential than attending to their cognitive development.

It is difficult for teachers to see the educative value of activities like lunch and recess because in almost all public schools they are structured in a bureaucratic fashion, constructed more like they are in prisons and factories than the way they are experienced in homes. Children take lunch and recess en masse; the activity and setting are impersonal and the children are anonymous; the activity is robbed of its personal, human element. But what if lunch occurred in the classroom with the teacher, a time for relaxed interchange? What if school resources and organization allowed teachers to have lunch and recess with children as well as time away from the classroom for other responsibilities, planning, or socializing with other adults?

As Golin explains, the issue of "non-pedagogical" responsibilities was a critical factor in the second strike in Newark, and the union leadership's insistence on holding on to a victory in arbitration that released teachers from these jobs pitted the union against community activists. The union's most persuasive argument in organizing elementary school teachers was that unionism made teacher professionalism possible by improving teachers' salary and working conditions. It would elevate their status and in so doing make teaching more like "work" and less like "home." But this definition of "professionalism" reinforced a conception of teachers' work that led in short order to internecine conflicts with black parents. Some teachers, however, understood teaching's worth in its being of service to families and neighborhoods, and, in other words, wanted teaching to transcend the dichotomy between "work" and "home." As Golin quotes one black parent observing, these "non-professional" chores were "the only human aspect of teaching" (p. 116). And in one alternative school Golin describes, a school in which parents and teachers had a strong working relationship, the issue of "non-professional" responsibilities was moot because lunch was a communal activity.

Two High Points

The book contains too much that is intelligent, informative, and moving to summarize. It must be read, but I will mention two high points for me. One often reads about "white workers" as if they are indistinguishable from one another. Golin's analysis of how the ideologies of the Italian American and Jewish teachers diverged and how the differences influenced the union's formation and demise demonstrates that the categorization "white workers" masks critically important differences as well as similarities. He also gets at how the black teachers who joined the union understood their commitment, how they made sense of being black and being workers. Golin's work is evidence that we can understand people's motivations and thinking as they are influenced by ethnicity, class, gender, and race without recourse to the jargon so often used in academic studies of these topics and without reference to the notion of "culture," which at least in educational research is the primary lens for explaining the phenomena Golin addresses as a historian.

The most dramatic part of the book is the discussion of the second strike and the description of the escalating violence, which threatened to explode in race war. Despite the excitement of this chapter, for me the most moving section of the book was the chapter in which he describes and analyzes the ways that the teacher activists faced their long prison sentences. Golin shows how the worldviews that configured their involvement in the union did the same in prison. For some women this meant organizing to change conditions, forming relationships with the black prisoners, starting classes, understanding the intentional brush of a leg as the expression of human desire for warmth and comfort rather than as a threatening lesbian advance.

For one teacher, Alice Saltman, an artist, jail was the occasion for meditation and drawing. The sketch of her cell is reproduced. In contrast, for the men jail was a competition, a test of their masculinity and a measure of how they stacked up against their jailer-opponents.

As Golin recounts these stories we see how each person struggled to feel human in this most barbaric environment. I think that most readers of *New Politics* will agree with me that it is close to impossible to read this chapter without identifying with their struggle, along with a feeling of great sadness that their sacrifice followed the defeat of their union and vision.

Golin ends the book with a hopeful look at the Newark Teachers Union today, which underwent eclipse and suffered from corruption in the '70s and '80s. He links the union's decline to the withering of its democratic traditions shortly after it won collective bargaining, which also occurred in New York City. (In fact, the comparison between what occurred in Newark and New York City is suggested but not explored so often in this study that it seems impossible that it will not be undertaken in a subsequent study, by someone else if not by Golin himself.) The Newark Teachers Union has a new president, one of the activists who helped build it, Joe Del Grosso.

Golin is reassured that the union is now heading in the right direction because Del Grosso emphasizes the importance of union democracy and participation of the membership. But I am less confident that the definition of "union democracy" that Del Grosso projects and Golin accepts is sufficient to heal the union's relations with Newark residents. First, there is no explicit mention of race and how this continues to influence the way teachers in Newark view their work and their union. Del Grosso's analysis of how the union should proceed, as Golin presents it, gives no indication that the union has come to grips with the contradictions that arise for teacher unions in the construction of "school" as a workplace that has no connection to home or family. Just as critically, although the generation of teachers who created the union is now starting to retire, the issue of race has not disappeared with the passage of time or the departure of the activists who built the union. Race and the way it influences one's view of schools, teaching, and teacher unions is still the "elephant in the closet" for teacher unionism in Newark and in most cities.

I saw an ominous indication of what is in store for the Newark Teachers Union, despite Joe Del Grosso's hopes, in a class I taught last year. Several young Newark teachers, all African American, born long after the story Golin narrates, were taking the course to complete their certification as principals. When we discussed teacher unionism, reading an inspirational speech by Margaret Haley about why teachers should organize, they expressed enthusiasm for her arguments about the need to reduce class size, about the critical importance of education in and for a democracy, about teachers having an alliance with other working people. As I always do when using this speech, I asked my students how their own union compared to Haley's vision. The tenor of the discussion shifted abruptly. Of the five young teachers in the class, only one had ever attended a union meeting, to find out about benefits. She presented the fact of her attendance at a union meeting as almost accidental and indicated that she would not return to another. The business of the union seemed irrelevant to her main concern, the quality of children's education. She made another comment that sent a chill down my back, even before I read Golin's book and learned how savage and bitter the racial divide in Newark had been during the second strike. "You know," she said, "I never knew there were so many white teachers in Newark." All the other African American teachers who worked in Newark nodded in agreement, a young male adding, "Yeah, you only see them at union meetings."

For union democracy to be real in the Newark Teachers Union and other unions as well, it can't be discussed in a race-free fashion. The union has to understand, as Golin does, that teachers are a varied group who want many different things from their union, some of which are contradictory. One of the main tensions is that the work that teachers do is not esteemed or valued by the dominant society in good part because it is "women's work." As Golin's book demonstrates, if those of us who support the struggles of all workers for dignity don't put race and gender on the table, our enemies will, and they will be joined by people who should be our allies.

10.

"Neoliberalism, Teacher Unionism, and the Future of Public Education"

First published in New Politics *10, no. 2, whole #38 (Winter 2005).*

With overwhelming support from both Democrats and Republicans, the Bush administration rewrote the Elementary and Secondary Education Act (ESEA) in 2001, drastically changing public education. One of the key initiatives of the Johnson-era "war on poverty," ESEA has been the main source of federal aid to schools serving children in poverty. Employing the rhetoric of "equity," the legislative package called "No Child Left Behind" (NCLB), has made federal aid dependent on schools accepting new regulations on a host of school policies, from teacher qualifications, to instructional content and methods permissible for reading instruction, to the privatization of school services, like tutoring. However, the mandates that have received the most attention require testing in grades three to eight and the reporting of disaggregated test scores for minority groups who have traditionally been "left behind" by schools, as well as by students identified as requiring special education. Schools that fail to deliver high test scores for all groups are publicly identified as failing and are subject to a host of punitive measures. Although there is much else in the package that affects all public schools that accept ESEA funds, testing and score reporting are the features of NCLB that are most hotly debated, in part because they affect *all* schools, everywhere, and not just those that are assumed to be "failing," (for example, city schools with high concentrations of poor, minority children).

The rhetorical premise of NCLB is that the federal government will finally hold public schools throughout the nation accountable for their failure to educate poor and working-class Hispanic and African American students. In this article, I explain how NCLB's purported aim of increasing educational opportunity masks its key purpose: to create a privatized system of public education that has a narrow, vocationalized curriculum enforced through use of standardized tests. I analyze the origins of support for some of NCLB's key premises and explain why the most prominent liberal criticism of NCLB, the underfunding of its provisions, is dangerously misleading, for both strategic and ideological reasons. Finally, I suggest how we might develop a progressive program and movement for school improvement, one connected to a revitalized teacher union and labor movement.

Bipartisan Backing

One aspect of NCLB mostly ignored by its opponents is that it both perpetuates and significantly deepens policies begun under George

H. W. Bush and continued by the Democrats and Bill Clinton. Yet, the origins of NCLB in educational reforms begun a decade earlier have been well documented. Writing in the *Educational Researcher* in November 1996, Gary Natriello noted that the bipartisan National Education Summit diverted attention away from many pressing problems in the US economy and its schools in a policy statement presenting high academic standards as a panacea. Describing the marketization of education in North Carolina in *Anthropology and Education Quarterly* in 2002, researchers identified intensified race and class stratification that resulted from policies implemented during the Clinton administration. Clinton pressed hard for Bush's National Goals 2000 and its emphasis on national standards enforced through standardized testing, and looked to his corporate allies for direction in setting education policy.

NCLB sharply divided the weakened traditional labor-liberal coalition that generally works together to win increases in school funding. The Council of Chief State School Officers, the Council of Great City Schools, and one teachers union, the American Federation of Teachers (AFT), which represents teachers in cities, supported the rationale that holding schools to "high standards" enforced through yearly standardized tests, with severe penalties for poor performance would force schools to shape up. The National Education Association (NEA) led the opposition to NCLB, arguing that its punitive sanctions, the absence of significant new funding, and the testing mandates were dangerous and destructive to public schools. The NEA is much larger than the AFT, and though it frequently cooperates with organized labor, it is not affiliated with the AFL-CIO. In its opposition to NCLB the NEA was joined by the American Association of School Administrators

(AASA), which represents some fourteen thousand superintendents and local administrators and major civil rights organizations including the NAACP (National Association for the Advancement of Colored People), as well as most progressive advocacy groups.

NCLB's rhetoric and its provisions that require reporting disaggregated test scores are enormously seductive to parents and low-income communities whose children attend poorly funded, poorly functioning schools. Schools in predominately Hispanic and African American neighborhoods are often incapable of providing children with more than the rudiments of literacy and numeracy—if that. Often these schools cannot recruit and retain sufficient numbers of teachers to staff classrooms. City and rural schools that enroll large concentrations of recent immigrants are frequently so underfunded and overwhelmed by the sheer numbers of students that bathrooms and closets are pressed into use as classrooms. Even in better-funded school districts in which African American and Hispanic youth are a demographic minority, they are frequently tracked into classes that offer a diet of low-level materials and poor instruction, robbed of the opportunity to take college preparatory work. African American boys are placed into special education in numbers vastly disproportionate to their presence in the school population. Once students are labeled as having "special needs," they are rarely given the help they need to move into regular programs, although this is the presumed rationale for identifying their problem and grouping them together.

For many years, schools' and school districts' test scores, graduation rates, and other statistical indicators commonly used to measure achievement, have been made public. However, in many states, New York for example, reports of test scores did not break down the achievement for different groups of children. A school would report the demographics of its student body and its passing rates on standardized tests, but it did not previously have to sort out, or disaggregate, the data so that correlations between achievement and demographics could be made. For this reason, inequality of achievement was often masked. Given school practices and conditions that allow millions of minority children to be undereducated, NCLB's requirement for disaggregated test reports and its "get tough" stance to punish schools that fail to help minority youth are attractive to many parents, most especially those who feel powerlessness to make institutions that are publicly funded serve their children adequately.

Note, too, that NCLB's passage follows on the failure of the civil rights movement's reforms to equalize educational opportunity. A full analysis of what occurred and why for the past thirty years of school reform would take me far beyond analysis of NCLB, but it is important to understand that NCLB's stated goal to "leave no child behind" would have far less popular resonance if schools presently served poor children of color reasonably well. NCLB's hijacking of the rhetoric of progressive educational reform would not be possible had progressive intentions to improve schooling been actualized, and so a brief explanation of what went wrong is needed. A radical vision of improved schooling for *all* children was lost in a Faustian bargain negotiated by legislators and bureaucrats, one embodied in the legislation creating ESEA. Relatively small infusions of public funds were given to schools and targeted at specific students, those presumed to need extra help, based on their family income, or in the case of bilingual education, their native language.

The funding's efficacy was measured by standardized tests, given at the beginning and end of each school year to students enrolled in classes that had materials and teachers paid for by ESEA monies. These "compensatory" programs ushered in the first widespread use of standardized test scores to measure teaching and learning, accepted as valid measures of whether public funds on education were being well spent. The model assumed that poor, minority children were not achieving because they—and their families—were deficient. It ignored, indeed contradicted, evidence of racism's destructive and systemic influences on how children are taught and what they are expected to know, as well as the bureaucratic organization of schooling.

Historically, public education in this country has coped with demands to equalize educational outcomes by blaming lack of achievement on students' individual problems, labeling their deficiencies, and then putting them in separate programs that "meet their needs." Our present policies for classifying students as having various sorts of educational disabilities differ primarily in nomenclature from those developed at the turn of the nineteenth century, when working-class students disinterested in school would be labeled "anemic" or "phlegmatic" and shunted into separate classes or schools.

NCLB definitively breaks this pattern by presuming that if children are not succeeding in school, responsibility rests with the school—and not the children. But in so doing, it destroys the structure and organization of a publicly funded and ostensibly publicly controlled system of education begun more than a century ago. NCLB closely resembles the blueprint developed in ultra-right-wing think tanks to replace locally controlled school systems funded by the states with a collection of privatized services governed only by the market. What NCLB adds to the original "free market" framework is the demand for standardized curricula and testing, and the Christian Right's press for "faith-based" interventions in public services.

NCLB's "free market" underpinning pretends that schools can compensate for the array of savage economic and social problems that undercut children's school success, problems created and abetted by government policies. In this mad reasoning, public funding for low-cost housing is cut back or eliminated. When the market's failure to provide adequate housing is evident in soaring rates of homelessness, schools are told that children's homelessness and its attendant social and logistical problems are no excuse for their failing scores on standardized tests. If there is sufficient political furor because of the obvious inability of schools to cope with this new crisis, the government creates a discrete, token allocation for homeless children. Often the money can't be used well, or perhaps at all, because the amount provided is so small relative to the enormity of the problems the school must overcome to provide meaningful assistance. Just tracking the whereabouts of children who move from one shelter to another, let alone providing them with appropriate services, is beyond the capacity of most urban school systems, which must interact with a number of similarly bureaucratic, under-resourced, and dysfunctional agencies.

NCLB draws on and encourages the powerful political mythology touted consistently in the media that schooling is the most effective way to overcome social inequality. This notion persists despite the overwhelming evidence that our educational system reproduces existing social relations. For this reason, any program to advance educational opportunity has to be understood as part of a larger project of attacking inequality with other social policies, including an end to de facto school segregation.

To argue that schools have a limited capacity to ameliorate economic and social inequality is not to diminish the moral or political importance of the struggle to improve education. Any progressive movement deserving of the name will demand that public schools provide all students with an education that will allow them to be well-rounded, productive citizens, which includes the ability to compete for whatever well-paying jobs exist. Improving schools that serve poor and working-class youth can make a difference in the lives of some children, and for that reason alone, progressive school reform deserves our attention. Moreover, struggling to improve schools for all children has a critical political significance because it demands that American society make good on its democratic ideals, its pledge of equality. While being clear that improved schooling is a moral and political imperative, we need to state its limitations as a policy vehicle for making the society more equitable. As the authors of *Choosing Equality* (1986) note, education can challenge the tyranny of the labor market—but not eliminate it. Especially as neoliberal policies tighten their grip on governments and capitalism's assault on the living conditions of working people intensifies, schooling becomes as an ever-weaker lever for improving the economic well being of individuals even while it remains a critical arena for political struggle.

The heart of any agenda for progressive social change, which includes improving education, must address what historian David Hogan terms "the silent compulsion of economic relations," the nexus of racial segregation in schools and housing, combined with dependence on local property taxes for school funding. Segregation in housing has become the pretext for abandoning the challenge of racially integrating schools, and segregation has seriously weakened the forces challenging funding inequities. Some African American activists and researchers advocate dropping the demand for integrating schools because the society has turned its back on its commitments to educate African American children, and they would be better served in segregated schools staffed by African American teachers. Arguing that we must attack the problems of segregated schools as they are today and not wait for integration to occur is different from substituting the former for the latter.

Although the despair that underlies desertion of the goal of integration is understandable, it fuels the erroneous romanticization of segregated schooling and ignores the reality that racially segregated schools and school systems are more isolated politically for being racially segregated and, thus, more vulnerable in funding battles in state legislatures. The urgency of making segregated schools better is undeniable, but so is the necessity of mounting a political and legal challenge both to the de facto segregation of schools *and* the use of local property taxes for schooling. Activists who lived through the busing battles of the 1970s, even those who have read about them, do not want to take up an issue that can incite vicious racism, but as racism underlies much of the opposition to funding schools serving poor, minority students adequately, it must be confronted. Unfortunately, even Ralph Nader's school reform plank (votenader.org), skirts this issue. While it observes that nationally school segregation has increased since the landmark decision in *Brown v. Board of Education*, the program does not call for desegregation but rather only for control of education to be left in the hands of the states with new investment in education. The federal government is identified as having a "critical supporting role" to ensure that all children, irrespective of family income or race are "provided with rich learning environments and equal educational opportunities." The platform rejects NCLB's focus on high-frequency, high-stakes, standardized testing as detrimental to children's intellectual and psychological well being, noting that it "is unfair to poorer children from devastating backgrounds."

There is much that is important in the statement on school reform on the Nader/Camejo website, for instance, its rejection of vouchers and corporate influences on curricula. Still, the absence of explicit attention to connections between racial segregation in schools and housing and state dependence on local property taxes for school funding is disappointing. Without making the case that segregation, school funding, and school quality are inextricably connected to one another, the argument against NCLB, especially in minority communities, is far less persuasive.

While NCLB's passage partly results from the Right's heightened political presence generally, its allure is also attributable to public confusion about defending a system of public education that seems to be unreformable. The tune played by both Democrats and Republicans is that Americans must scale back their expectations about governmental responsibility for services now portrayed as individual and personal concerns, like housing and health care. Both parties now insist that American society cannot fulfill its promise of providing equal *educational* opportunity. As Nader points out, NCLB's passage is also a dismaying indication of the degree of popular disorientation about the role of education in a democracy and the contradiction of privatizing an essential civic function.

The New Agenda

The overwhelming support by both Democrats and Republicans for NCLB is explained in part by the generally submissive stance of the Democratic Party to Republican initiatives. However, bipartisan endorsement of a legislative package that contains such disparate, and for liberals, politically repugnant regulations, deserves a closer look. After all, NCLB contains much that contradicts basic premises of liberal capitalism in the past fifty years, including the evaporation of separation of church and state (NCLB allows religious organizations to provide after-school services and requires that classes in sex education consist of exhortations for abstinence). And yet, the Democratic Party embraced NCLB, wholeheartedly, with Bush singling out Ted Kennedy for praise for the assistance Kennedy gave in its passage.

According to the Constitution, education is a responsibility of the states, and in theory states could refuse to comply with NCLB by refusing ESEA funds. Despite a few threats to do so, no state has yet turned its back on ESEA funds because schools in revenue-poor districts, which also have students who are the most expensive to educate, would be financially devastated. The state government would be obliged to craft a rescue. As is obvious from the protracted legal battles to equalize state funding, there is little political will on the state level to give low-wealth/high-need school districts the funding they need and deserve.

Why, then, were liberals and moderates in both parties so willing to support a legislative package with these (and other) equally regressive provisions? The glue that held together the bipartisan endorsement of NCLB is the shared ideological support for neoliberalism's program for the global capitalist economy, a global transformation in education's character and role.[1] NCLB enacts the program for education that neoliberal economists and governments pursue internationally. In both industrialized nations and the developing world, neoliberal reforms are promoted as rationalizing and equalizing delivery of social services. Toward this end, the World Bank demands curricular and structural change in education when it provides loans. The "wish list" is seen in the draft version of the *World Development Report 2004: Making Services Work for Poor People* (WDR 2004), which describes education's purpose solely in terms of preparing workers for jobs in a global economy: Reformed educational systems will allow transnational capitalism to move jobs whenever and wherever it wishes, that is, to the country with the working conditions and salaries that are worst for workers and best for profits.[2]

The draft was later modified in negotiations with governments and nongovernmental organizations, but the original version is a declaration of war on every aspect of the social contract, especially provision of pubic education and the existence of teachers unions. Public education remains the largest realm of public expenditures that is highly unionized and not yet privatized, and the draft report identifies *unions*, especially teachers unions, as one of the greatest *threats* to global prosperity. The draft argues that unions have "captured governments," holding poor people hostage to their demands for more pay. The report combines a savage attack on teachers and teacher unions, including a suggestion that they should be fired wholesale when they strike or otherwise resist demands for reduced pay, with a call to privatize services, greatly reduce public funding, devolve control of schools to neighborhoods, and increase user fees. The World Bank has implemented many elements of the draft report by making loans and aid contingent on "restructuring," that is, destroying publicly funded, publicly controlled educational systems. The results, including reduced literacy rates, have been devastating, as University of Buenos Aires professor Adriana Puiggros describes in her report contrasting the reality of implementation in Argentina with the World Bank's rhetoric of equality.[3]

A key element of the program is limiting access to higher education through the imposition of higher tuition and reduced government support to both institutions and individual students. Limiting access to higher education means lower education needs only to prepare students for work, the jobs requiring basic skills that multinationals aim to move from one country to another. Schools that train most workers for jobs requiring limited literacy and numeracy, which *World Development Report 2004* explains is all we can realistically expect for poor people in poor countries, does not require teachers who are themselves well educated or skilled as teachers. In fact, teachers who have a significant amount of education are a liability because they are costly to employ; teacher salaries are the largest expense of any school system. Minimally educated workers require only teachers who are themselves minimally educated, and so teacher education is eliminated or deskilled in the neoliberal program.

Most of NCLB's elements for reorganizing education in the United States are straight out of the draft report for *World Development Report 2004*. Charter schools (and the Bush administration's not-yet-realized plan for vouchers to be used in private schools) fragment oversight and control; testing requirements and increasingly punitive measures for low test scores pressure schools to limit what is taught so that the tests become the curriculum; privatization of school services, like tutoring and professional development for teachers—tied to raising test scores—undercuts union influence and membership. NCLB's definition of a "highly qualified" teacher actually deskills teaching because it assumes that all one needs to know to teach well is content in the liberal arts. NCLB further limits which content knowledge teachers need by eliminating majors that are more likely to promote teaching's nurturing functions, psychology and sociology, or a critique of social relations, as one generally finds in the newer disciplines associated with the social movements that spawned them, like black or women's studies.

In several states teachers can become "highly qualified" by presenting a BA and a passing score for an online exam of teaching that Chester Finn developed with a 35-million-dollar grant from the Bush administration. The hysterically anti-union politics of the draft report also explain the remark by Rod Paige, secretary of the Department of Education, that the NEA is a "terrorist organization." Although his remark was dismissed as a bizarre joke, it echoes the tone of the draft report. The president of the AFT local in Houston with whom Paige had collaborated before coming to Washington was almost alone in defending Paige publicly, commenting to the *Washington Post* that Paige was really quite a wonderful fellow, his joke was harmless, and that the NEA wasn't even a real union, let alone a terrorist organization. (I was curious as to whether she had been quoted accurately, and so I contacted her for a clarification. Sadly, she was.)

The Bush administration is quite open about the explicit linkage between a deskilled teaching force and a narrow curriculum, a fact that is, tellingly, not publicized by Democratic supporters of the legislation, even or especially those who want only to fund it better. Grover Whitehurst, undersecretary in what was formerly the US Department of Education and is now the Institute of Education Sciences (though its blind fealty to the doctrines of market capitalism and Christian fundamentalism mock its pretensions to scientific research), explained in a meeting with educational researchers that public investment in teacher education is unnecessary because the government is required to provide only a basic education that will prepare students for entry-level jobs. Therefore, government funds are better spent creating materials for teaching basic skills that teachers with little or no expertise in teaching can use. This is precisely the strategy promoted in *World Development Report 2004*, which lauds programs that briefly train fifteen-year-old peasant girls, who then teach literacy skills in rural villages.

One way to limit access is charging fees and tuitions to attend school, in both lower and higher education. We see the former strategy in underdeveloped countries, where families must often pay for schooling that was once available for free. In fact, a World Bank policy *prohibited* provision of free education as a requirement for loans, until a movement by liberals in the US Congress, informed and inspired by global justice activists, challenged this measure. Access to learning is also limited by limiting what is learned. Larry Kuehn, research director of the British Columbia Teachers Federation, has traced this process and begins the trail in Washington in 1987, in the Reagan administration, when the United States promoted development of "education indicators" to guide curricula and testing at the Organization for Economic Cooperation and Development (OECD), an organization of the twenty-nine most industrialized countries and some rapidly industrializing nations, like Korea and Mexico. In these early discussions, the OECD planned how to develop uniform curricula with "culture-free" materials, appropriate for the new "information economy." Kuehn's work illuminates not only the anti-intellectual and antihumanistic assumptions of these curricula, but also how existing expectations about what students should learn had to be "downscaled."

The National Assessment of Educational Progress (NAEP), a federal agency that monitors academic achievement, works with the OECD. In the United States, the NAEP has traditionally assessed students' achievements in three sorts of reading: "reading for literary experience," "reading to be informed," and "reading to perform a task." However, the OECD determined that only one ability, "reading to perform a task," as measured for example by reading a computer manual, would be used in international assessments of student learning. Testing the ability to read for literary experience was rejected as being too difficult to assess because of cross-cultural differences. The decision to limit the reading assessment to "reading to perform a task" and the example of this skill illustrates transnational capitalism's intention to redefine education as vocational training.

Teacher Unionism

As Puiggros notes in her description of education's restructuring in Argentina and throughout Latin America, resistance has been led by teacher unions. In organizing this struggle, teacher union activists have paid a hefty price: firings, beatings, even assassination. While both the AFT and NEA have offered statements of support to these heroic unionists, their public pronouncements and letter-writing campaigns are undercut and contradicted by political allegiances and ideological beliefs that reinforce much of the neoliberal program.

The two unions differ in important ways that I analyze below, but the starting point for understanding their response to the neoliberal assault is that they see the world in US-centric terms. More specifically, their vision of the world is refracted through the eyes of capitalist hegemony. The NEA's faulty vision results from ideological backwardness, a failure it can indulge because unlike the unionists in the countries receiving the World Bank "largesse," teachers in the United States have been relatively protected from the program the United States enforces on the rest of the world. In contrast, the AFT leadership takes a more sympathetic view of the neoliberal project and seeks to position itself as a partner institution in the neoliberal agenda.

Although Albert Shanker, the AFT's longtime chief, died in 1997, his organizational stranglehold on the union, his political compact with social conservatives, and his leadership of the segment of the AFL-CIO that has collaborated with the US government in subverting popular movements throughout the globe, were continued by his cothinker and replacement, Sandra Feldman, who recently resigned the AFT presidency due to poor health.[4] The similarities between Shanker's vision for school reform, which because of his ironclad control of the union was de facto that of the organization, and the neoliberal program manifested in NCLB are apparent in his article, published posthumously, in the *Forum for Applied Research and Public Policy*.

If we ignore the article's curmudgeonly tone and focus on its content, Shanker's agreement with the major portion of the neoliberal educational program is apparent. First, Shanker contends that US schools are far worse than those in OECD nations because we offer *too much* access to higher education, or as he formulates the problem, we have an insufficient amount of academic "tracking." We don't start early enough to put students into programs that prepare them for their vocational destinies, so he advocates putting all students into vocational tracks some time between grades five and nine. In their earlier grades, they should have a curriculum based on E. D. Hirsch's project for "cultural literacy." Although he maintains that in these tracks students must all be held to "high standards," his use of Hirsch's curriculum signifies that instead of engaging firsthand with primary sources, reading, appreciating, and perhaps creating literature, students will memorize facts about the "great" (white male) figures of history, the arts, and science. He bemoans the absence of a system of high-stakes tests with really harsh penalties for failure, the absence of mandatory national curriculum standards, and the presence of far too much tolerance for student misconduct. Shanker assails the laxity of the pre-NCLB curriculum standards, which were additionally problematic for being left to the states to execute.

Shanker adds that some standards can be too "vague for example, 'Learn to appreciate literature.'" Shanker's breezy dismissal of the standard about appreciating literature echoes the OECD's rejection of international assessment in "reading for literary experience." Shanker used his weekly column in the *New York Times*, paid for by the membership, to ridicule the national standards developed by professional organizations of teachers of the arts, rejecting them as grandiose and unrealistic, though his own children attended school in a suburban district with excellent arts programs—and no E. D. Hirsch curricula.

Union members had not formally endorsed many of the positions Shanker adopted, for instance rejection of the standards in the arts. Recent surveys of teachers, in cities, suburbs, and rural schools find even less support now than there was at the time Shanker advocated many of his positions about standards and testing. Yet because of the AFT's bureaucratic deformation, of which the indictments for graft in the Miami and Washington, DC, locals are shamefully graphic illustrations, the opposition to the AFT's vocal, unwavering support for testing and "high standards" scarcely registers at the national level. Most of the biggest locals are so bureaucratic that rank-and-file challenges to the leadership must be about fundamental practices of democracy in order to allow classroom teachers' voices on issues of educational policy to be heard.

The NEA generally can be counted on to adopt liberal positions on the important political issues of the day, although its positions do not necessarily represent those of its members because its organizational structure is also bureaucratic but in a different way from the AFT. The AFT is a federation of locals so the state organizations have small staffs and little power. The AFT constitution contains no term limits for its president who has little direct control of local functions. Shanker masterfully exploited the post of AFT president to promote himself and to trumpet his political views on a wide range of opinions. He did so by using his domination of the massive New York City local to leverage control of the national organization and ensuring that his political views received a formal stamp of approval from the union's executive council but were never debated at the local level. Shanker ruled the national staff with an iron fist ideologically, employing only people who agreed with him—or were fired.

In contrast, power in the NEA resides with the state organizations. Presidents of the national organization are usually career teachers who have been active in the state affiliates. They are limited to two terms, a fact that encourages staff control of operations and policy. In the AFT, dues remain in the locals so that they hire their own organizers directly. In the NEA, dues go to the state affiliate, which hires organizers, who are then assigned to work for locals as the needs arise. Thus NEA's organizational structure puts the staff in the political saddle, and the politics of its staff resemble those found in other public employee unions in the United States, like AFSCME and SEIU, generally left leaning. While the NEA is better positioned than the AFT to lead a struggle in this country for progressive school reform, it is hampered by its own bureaucratic structure and its roots as a professional organization controlled by school administrators: It moved to become a collective bargaining agent only after the AFT's stunning successes in organizing city teachers into unions in the 1960s and 1970s forced it to do so.

As with other left-leaning public employee unions, the NEA is willing to be openly critical of the use of US military and political force to safeguard capitalism in a way that the AFT is not. Perhaps in part because of its roots as a professional organization, the NEA lacks the ideological sophistication of other progressive unions in the United States and of its counterparts in Europe that are connected to social democratic parties. The NEA is clearly trying to make ideological sense of the global attack against teacher unionism and public education, searching unsuccessfully for a vocabulary—and lever—for resistance. At bottom, the NEA fails to understand the premise of Daniel Singer's work, *Whose Millennium?* (Monthly Review Press, 1999): The struggles today do not result from changes in "technology" or "globalization," which are phenomena advanced to mask the real culprit, capitalism's structural crisis and its neoliberal "solutions." The chief ideological impediment to developing a resistance is acceptance of TINA, the notion that "There Is No Alternative" (TINA) to capitalism and its destructive policies. The NEA's failure to name the problem has kept it from generating a class-conscious, anticapitalist critique that would guide development of the program needed to derail NCLB and the neoliberal program for education.

The NEA and AFT are by far the biggest member organizations in the Educational International (EI), the international confederation of teacher unions, which is affiliated with the other international organizations of unions, like the Trade Union Advisory Committee to the OECD. The EI seems to "agree to disagree," that is, not take a position or action on issues on which its most powerful members, the AFT and NEA, dissent—either with one another or with the other delegates, especially those from developing countries who are feeling the brunt of the neoliberal policies formulated and pressed by the United States. The EI's evasion of critical issues of war and peace, like the Israeli-Palestinian crisis and the war in Iraq, is possible primarily because it is comprised of national union leaders. Then–General Secretary Fred van Leeuwen remarked at its Third World Congress in 2001:

> One of the strengths of the Education International is that we are a genuine membership-based organization. Some 80 percent of our members are involved in policy development and decision-making processes. An impressive figure. But this percentage is made up of no more than approximately 2,000 individuals . . . who speak for EI's 24 million members. Most classroom teachers in the North have never heard of EI, and that is a bit worrisome. We run the risk of becoming a club of union leaders and their international secretaries. Don't misinterpret my words. Those 2,000 EI activists are our life and blood. But we must, I believe, find ways to open our gates to your members and enable them, where possible, to take part in our work. Teachers are world citizens by nature; they are among the most active members of organizations like Amnesty,

Greenpeace, and other NGOs. Why not find ways to get them
involved in their own organization?[5]

The AFT flexes its muscle by influencing the EI's functioning
informally, through private discussions with the general secretary
of the organization, rather than in open debate at its international
conferences and congresses. The NEA has traditionally been reluctant to express any opinion related to US foreign policy. Fortunately,
the AFT has lost many of its contacts with other member organizations and it continues to be regarded by the social-democratic
teacher unions in Europe with suspicion, and rightly so because of
its well-documented involvement with US military and political
repression of democratic, anticapitalist struggles.[6]

EI minutes and official statements, posted on its website, reveal
an organization that is struggling to make sense of the attack on public education and unions. It has been slow to mobilize beyond the
stage of working with other international labor organizations in is-
suing public appeals and organizing letter-writing campaigns when
teacher unionists are brutalized. Its efforts in this regard are ad-
mirable, for instance, the campaign to free Taye Woldesmiate, president of the Ethiopian Teacher Association, who has spent six years
in prison, and its publicity about Colombian teachers being killed
and exiled for union activity. However, the advocacy on behalf of individual unionists is undercut by the unwillingness to name the real
enemy, the US-backed economic and political neoliberal agenda.

To the extent the EI focuses on isolated outrages rather than
identifying these abuses as manifestations of capitalism's current
disregard for human needs that interfere with its appetite for un-
limited profits, the EI campaigns allow the AFT to cover its trail
of complicity with the US government's subversion of popular

movements by printing a blurb in its newspaper about individual militants who need support. Without advocacy about individual abuses being linked to efforts to build a broad, militant international social movement that challenges capitalism's demands for privatization, defunding, and fragmentation of educational services, the NEA too can more easily continue to deny the implications of US control over policies at the World Bank.

In the last year especially, the EI has begun to mobilize in promising ways. It joined the Global Campaign for Education, a broad alliance of NGOs, child rights activists, and teachers' organizations active in more than 150 countries, to forcefully challenge the draft report's analysis and conclusions.[7] Unlike the tepid, polite statement issued by TUAC defending the importance of teachers unions and labor unions in general,[8] the Global Campaign for Education tapped the vitality and language of the global justice movement. The EI has brought teacher unionism into a coalition with the defenders of the oppressed rather than the oppressors, a stance that is continued with its participation in "Global Action Week 2005," a continuation of the work of the Global Campaign for Education. EI now has an advocacy team that collaborates with the Public Services International in producing the *Tradeducation News*, with updates about global resistance to the inclusion of education as a commodity to be traded in the world treaties being pressed by the United States.[9]

Restructuring Education

In comparing the draft and final versions of *World Development Report 2004* the successes of the international coalition EI helped to forge are clear. The vitriolic attack on teacher unions was diminished to a mild criticism for them not to be too self-interested. The glowing examples of teachers being fired for striking were removed. The original focus on the unions as enemies of poor people was replaced with arguments that sound like they are taken from (conservative) political science textbooks about the "long route" and "short route" to governmental accountability. And in July 2004, a senior vice president of the World Bank was invited to address the EI Congress in Porto Alegre, Brazil. He extolled the role of teachers in economic development, noting the vital nature of partnership with teachers unions and with the EI. He commented that when the top officials from Education International met with World Bank president James Wolfensohn in December (about the draft report that attacked teachers and teacher unions), they had "an open, frank dialogue about how best to support teachers."[10]

I learned about the meeting between Wolfensohn and EI officials at a panel I chaired at a meeting of educational researchers in April 2004, one in which Mary Hatwood Futrell, the immediate past president of the EI and a past president of NEA, spoke. She was joined by Larry Kuehn, whose research on globalization on behalf of the British Columbia Teachers Federation is the closest substitute we have for the advocacy research the US teachers unions should be doing,[11] and Hugo Aboites, a Mexican sociologist who works with Mexican teacher union activists in an alliance opposing the government-controlled unions. As Kuehn described the *World Development Report 2004* draft report assailing teacher unions as enemies of global prosperity, I took a liberty as chair and asked Kuehn to pause so that we could hear from both Futrell and Aboites on the issue. Futrell described the dismay of EI officials when they saw the report; how they called Wolfensohn immediately; how Wolfensohn denied knowledge of the report and said its viewpoint had not been officially sanctioned. I asked Futrell how she understood Wolfersohn's explanation and she fell silent, unable to answer. I then asked Aboites the same question, and he said he did not know of this particular report, but he was familiar with the policies. Teacher unionists in Mexico are experiencing horrible attacks on their jobs, their unions, and their bodies when they resist, all under the watchful eye of the government—and the World Bank.

As Fred van Leeuwen noted, teachers in the North have so far avoided learning about neoliberalism's global assault on education. With NCLB, they and we are now being subjected, albeit in a protected version, to the neoliberal program wreaking devastation elsewhere. When teacher union activists who opposed US suppression of popular resistance to authoritarian dictatorships in the 1980s tried to make their case, the job was difficult because even then the unions were bureaucratic. But in addition they struggled against the distance most US teachers feel from the world. Today our situation is changed. On September 11 the illusion that physical distance protects ordinary US citizens was shattered. With NCLB another self-deception has been challenged, the notion that teacher unions can deliver the "bottom line" of maintaining teachers' wages, benefits, and jobs without embracing a view of their purpose that makes them allies with social movements that challenge the status quo. Yet, still missing in the work of teacher unions, their leaders, and their ranks, is an understanding that to defend public education in this country, teachers and their unions must help develop an international response to neoliberalism, one that puts justice and equity at the forefront of the union's program for education, one that develops alliances that span national borders.

The sort of political work that is needed to awaken teachers and teacher unionists in this country to the global responsibility that comes with living in the belly of the imperial beast has begun, for instance, with the antiwar caucus formed at the AFT convention in August 2004. This activity encourages teacher unionists outside the United States, for instance, in the EI, to make the case in official organizations to which US unions belong, to name the enemy of public education correctly *not* as globalization, but as capitalist restructuring under a neoliberal program.

Any effective struggle against the neoliberal policies that are embedded in NCLB must battle the bipartisan consensus about TINA. Clearly that means creating an electoral vehicle that gives voice to real alternatives. Despite the flaws with Nader's stance on NCLB, the campaign's clear rejection of the Democratic and Republican Parties' agreement to reduce education to a system of job training, trashing education's political functions in a democracy, point in the right direction. This path leads to a difficult but undeniable conclusion: NCLB cannot be doctored up. It should not be better funded. It should be replaced with a legislative program that is characterized by "progressive federalism," a concept that was clearly defined in *Choosing Equality*, over twenty-five years ago.

That is a large order, but we can see the elements of the sort of struggle that's needed: in the work of advocacy groups that fought NCLB; in teachers unions' mobilization of community groups and parents to resist World Bank policies in Latin America and elsewhere; in the work of the EI and PSI (Public Services International) in their collaboration to develop global campaigns with advocacy and global justice organizations, which reject TINA. With "progressive federalism" we have a progressive program. What we need most immediately is for those who see the harm done by NCLB to recognize its political origins in the neoliberal project—and combat the project in its entirety. That requires the determination to reject the will of both political parties who advocate a system of education that leaves children and democracy behind capitalism's race for greater profits at any cost.

11.

"The (People's) Summit of the Americas"

First published in New Politics *10, no. 4, whole #40 (Winter 2006).*

On November 2–5, as two dozen heads of state gathered in Mar del Plata, Argentina, for a hemispheric summit to negotiate trade agreements, thousands of global justice activists, I among them, participated in a concurrent "People's Summit" ("*cumbre de los pueblos*") or "counter-summit" ("*contracumbre*"). The official summit meetings were moved to Mar del Plata, a seaside resort that is a five-hour bus or train trip from Buenos Aires, to deter mass protests. The ability of the global justice movement to bring thousands of contracumbre participants to Mar del Plata was testimony to the economic devastation neoliberal economic policies have produced in Latin America as well as to popular determination to resist further inroads in the quality of life. Most Argentinians watched their life savings and livelihoods vanish overnight with the devaluation of the peso, and Bush's presence at the summit was a bitter—and unwelcome—reminder of US domination in the World Bank and International Monetary Fund and the policies that led to the peso's devaluation.

I joined a Canadian contingent that traveled to the Educational Summit (*"cumbre educativa"*), held in conjunction with the People's Summit. My report is focused primarily on the Educational Summit because its sessions were concurrent with other workshops and meetings of the contracumbre. However, judging from the listing of sessions in the contracumbre program, as well as by the number of people at the contracumbre opening rally, the Educational Summit was the largest single gathering of the counter-summit. Organized by CTERA (Confederación de Trabajadores de la Educación de la República Argentina), the more left wing of the two confederations of teachers unions in Argentina, and supported by the labor confederation representing public employees, CTA (Central de Trabajadores de la Argentina), the Educational Summit brought together hundreds of activists.

As I've explained elsewhere,[1] public education in Latin America and much of the world is the battleground of a fierce struggle between progressive forces trying to maintain public systems of schooling, and on the other side, international financial institutions and neoliberal governments supported by the United States with a program that uses the rhetoric of educational equity to dismantle public education. To neoliberal politicians and transnational corporations, education is a huge, untapped market for supplies and services: standardized tests and curricula to train and sort the new global workforce; and online degrees supplied by corporations located mostly in Australia and the United States. The primary obstacle to neoliberalism's restructuring of education is teacher unions, which throughout Latin America and much of Africa have led popular struggles for free, universal public education as a social right. Teacher union leadership in the contracumbre and protests against Bush were quite visible. CTERA organized a work stoppage of teachers on November 5 to protest Bush's presence in Argentina and the assault on public education. The public employee confederation, CTA, of which it is a member, endorsed and joined the effort.

The *New York Times* coverage of the summit and the global justice meetings highlighted photos of protestors holding aloft images of Che Guevara, fiery anti-US rhetoric of Hugo Chávez, and the stalled "progress" by heads of state in reaching consensus on new trade agreements. Unsurprisingly, the *Times*'s analysis is simultaneously accurate and politically misleading. US media, as usual, did not explain the reasons for Bush's unpopularity, yet it would be difficult to overstate the harm done to the general standard of living in Latin America in the name of economic restructuring and free trade, promoted and enforced by the US government. From the friendly hand waves and shouts of support given demonstrators in the massive protest on the streets of Buenos Aires the day Bush arrived to the unsolicited encouragement I received from hotel clerks, taxi drivers, salespeople, and waiters when I mentioned my participation in the contracumbre, hostility to Bush and the expansion of free trade was deep and widely visible. Equally apparent from coverage of the summit by the Argentinean media was popular unease about the massive police and military presence in Mar del Plata. Police, often with machine guns, cordoned off the city into two sections. Only those with an official security clearance could travel into the section of Mar del Plata with the fancy hotels and official meetings. (With the exception of those ubiquitous machine guns, Mar del Plata's deployment of police was not that different from the police saturation around Madison Square Garden during the last Republican National Convention.) Argentinean discomfort with this show of armed force is more than understandable when one considers that the question of how to win justice for victims of the military's dirty war against the Left is still a passionate debate. The pages of *Página/12*, Argentina's left-leaning daily newspaper, regularly contain memorial announcements on the anniversary of the date on which people "disappeared." The photos of young students and statements from family and friends that they will not "forget or forgive" are a reminder of the democratically elected government's tenuous ability to navigate the righteous calls for justice and the unbroken back of the political forces responsible for the terror.

A network of Canadian and Latin American unions, called the Initiative for Democratic Education in the Americas (IDEA), used the occasion of the contracumbre and the Educational Summit to meet. The network has emerged slowly over the past decade, nurtured in North America mostly by progressives in the British Columbia Teachers Federation and Centrale des Syndicats du Québec (CSQ) and in Latin America by CTERA and a coalition of Mexican teachers unions that are independent of the corrupt government-controlled organizations. The Hemispheric Secretariat on Education, a broader umbrella group separate from the IDEA network, organized the Educational Summit along with CTERA, with support from the Latin American branch of the Education International (EI), the international confederation of teachers unions. Buses chartered by CTERA took its delegates and those of us in an international contingent for the five-hour bus ride from Buenos Aires to Mar del Plata. Activists, both working teachers who hold union office and full-time staff, came from Mexico, Ecuador (representing Chile and Bolivia), Nicaragua, Brazil, Uruguay, and the Caribbean. A Cuban delegate arrived independently. CTERA hosted the international visitors and its delegates at hotels it owned and operated, an arrangement dating back to Peronist days when unions held their conventions in Mar del Plata and rented the facilities out to union members when the hotel was not otherwise being used. Two other people from the United States traveled with the IDEA network, a filmmaker who recently completed a powerful new documentary *Granito de Arena* (*Grains of Sand*)[2] about the struggles of Mexican teachers unions, and a faculty member from Evergreen State College in Washington who more than a decade ago helped forge hemispheric cooperation to oppose neoliberal trade agreements.[3] I appeared to be the sole activist in a US teachers union at the IDEA network meetings and at the Educational Summit.

Despite my rudimentary Spanish, it was clear to me that the IDEA network contains representatives of organizations with sharp political differences. Representatives all listened respectfully to one another and also gingerly avoided pointed debates. Still, striking political disagreements emerged in delegates' presentations about the conditions in their respective countries in regard to educational policy and teacher union responses. The Mexicans, representing a network of opposition locals, distributed hand-folded photocopies of their ten-point program, materials that illustrated well the grassroots nature of their organization, which is battling the government and a party-controlled union. The Brazilian delegate described the "delicate" political situation of the teachers unions in working with the government it had helped bring to power based on promises that were being broken. Argentina's delegate discussed the school reform program of her teachers confederation CTERA but not that of the rival confederation, CEA, which like CTERA is an affiliate of the Education International. (CEA also participated in the Educational Summit but is not in the IDEA network.) Representatives from the Ecuador teachers union distributed books printed on heavy, glossy paper filled with color photos and sharp criticisms of capitalism. When they concluded their report with a call for revolution and the overthrow of capitalism, I surmised, correctly I learned later, that this union was affiliated with the Communist Party. Sitting in on the meeting, a US professor gave a brief report about the (sorry) state of the Left in the United States, explaining he lacked expertise to discuss US teachers unions.

A Hemispheric Network—Without the United States?

The contradiction in this being a *hemispheric* network, with representation of teachers unions in much of Latin America and Canada but not the United States, has been the topic of my conversations with Canadians. Latin American and Canadian teachers unions obviously should not and cannot delay organizing an alliance until US unions are ready to join them. But to the extent possible, given meager human and financial resources, attempts to involve US teachers unions should be an organizing priority. One purely practical reason to try to involve more US participants is that they can add resources and political contacts that can benefit the Latin American unions. Further, including US teacher-activists in the network would clarify that the attack on public education and the struggle of educational workers is not simply a struggle between the United States and the rest of the hemisphere. The absence of US participation encourages a national rather than class configuration to network politics, providing a smokescreen for the often willing collaboration of local plutocrats in neoliberal policies. An experience I had at the opening rally illustrated what might occur with more involvement by US teachers unions in the contracumbre. The exuberant CTERA activists sitting in front of me began chanting an equivalent of "Yankees go home!" Then they did a double-take when they realized I was behind them. They apologized for any offense they may have caused and I explained (I think) that I understood their chant as signaling political opposition to Bush, not to those of us in the United States who oppose him. Together we resumed waving CTERA banners, cheering, and chanting slogans.

In calling for greater involvement of US teachers unions, I should clarify that it must be based on the explicit, unequivocal rejection of the imperial appetite and policies of the US government. This is the sine qua non of any principled international alliance among unions. As I pointed out in my article cited above, the leadership of the American Federation of Teachers (AFT) generally identifies the greatest threat to education emanating from popular resistance to policies that shore up capitalism, and on many issues the AFT as a national organization is found on the *wrong* side of the literal and actual barricades that separate global justice activists from heads of state. One Canadian activist was incredulous when he learned that the AFT national leadership fully endorses standardized testing and helped draft many provisions of the Bush administration's omnibus education "reform," the No Child Left Behind Act. The absence of the other, larger US teachers union, the National Education Association (NEA), was something of a disappointment to conference organizers. At the last minute the

NEA decided it would not participate, officially or unofficially. The formal explanation was that Education International segments its North American and Caribbean affiliates in one sector and its Latin American affiliates in another. The NEA argued that its participation in a hemispheric meeting was counter to EI's organizational structure. The speciousness of this argument was readily exposed by the presence of EI's newly elected president and his prominent role in the Educational Summit. Plainly, the NEA's explanation masked other concerns, probably a sense of vulnerability to attack by the rival AFT. In domestic politics the NEA almost always takes positions that are more left-leaning than those advocated by the AFT. Participation in the Educational Summit and the IDEA network, especially given Cuba's prominence, would have made the NEA open to AFT charges that the NEA is "soft on communism," a criticism the NEA wants to avoid.

In the conference workshop on free trade, I decided to test political possibilities of developing a hemispheric collaboration that included the expression of disagreements. Realizing that as the sole activist from a US teachers union my remarks on any subject would be closely scrutinized for political implications, I commented on a subject I hoped would be less politically pointed, how teachers unions should regard online education. The World Bank and neoliberal governments internationally are pressing for teachers to be educated through online course work. Online education is an attractive option for neoliberal politicians as it can be provided cheaply by for-profits with use of contingent labor/faculty whose low wages ensure hefty profits. Requiring online coursework ignores how often teachers do not have ready access to the technology they need to complete online courses, as well as the need for social contact with colleagues that a traditional classroom environment provides. While defending the right of teachers to choose the learning environment that they find most helpful and arguing for equity in access to the technology, I also suggested that we should imagine the progressive potential of online learning, to consider how the technology could be a powerful pedagogical tool if used for public good rather than for profit. I suggested we could create online classes in which teachers in the hemisphere share knowledge and analysis and that, as this example illustrated, the exploitation of technologies for profit should not blind us to how we might harness such tools for *our* purposes.

A hailstorm of criticism followed my remarks. From the dais a Cuban student who had presented one of the workshop addresses dismissed my idea, averring that Cuba permits nothing but face-to-face instruction for its foreign language teaching because personal interaction is the only way learning can occur. Her passionate repudiation of technology contradicted what I subsequently learned: Canadian teachers who collaborate with Cuban school officials in a project to improve the teaching of foreign languages have been frustrated by the Cubans' unwillingness to end the (ineffective) practice of using video instruction for foreign language teachers. Despite many topics far more urgent than distance learning, debate in the workshop remain riveted on my incendiary notion that technology is a tool that could be used for social progress. (Plainly, delegates did not share Lenin's thinking that Electrification plus Soviets equals Communism.) Finally, a lone CTERA delegate observed that "political and economic situations" determine the use of any tool, and that technology is a tool. The moderator of the workshop, an experienced CTERA leader who had to formulate a consensus, ably constructed a platform statement that acknowledged my point as well as my critics' ideas.

The Educational Summit meetings and documents were marked by a passionate romance with Cuba. The Cuban delegation, a racially diverse group of exuberant young people attired in red jogging suits, thrived in the spotlight. Cuba's representative to the IDEA network was warmly embraced when she walked into a planning meeting a bit after work had begun. In his opening remarks to the Educational Summit, Thulas Nxesi, the gregarious EI president from South Africa's teachers union who follows in office Mary Futrell, former president of the NEA, gave his "special greeting to the Cuban people here today," noting their "very special place in our hearts." The "role they played in the liberation of Africa" has made them "a shining example of the left project and the new world order," he stated, to wild applause and cheers. In a pause after Nxesi's remarks, I turned to a genial delegate from the Canadian Teachers Federation seated next to me and asked what sense he made of these comments. The Canadian was plainly disconcerted by my question and responded that "we have to understand" that Cuba has given considerable support to Africa and "people are grateful." IDEA network publications also reflect the embrace of Cuba as a progressive alternative to neoliberalism. The IDEA network's report on democratic education in the Americas, written by the international secretary of the Peruvian Education Workers Union, extols Cuba's educational system as a model for the rest of Latin America, arguing that "With the exception of Cuba . . . [Latin American] education systems tend to be anti-democratic and elitist."

The shameful failure of US teachers unions to oppose unequivocally the menacing of Cuba by the United States and US-supported policies that are destroying public education in Latin America fuels the romance with Cuba. The embrace of Cuba similarly depresses prospects for organizing broad political support for the Hemispheric Secretariat and the IDEA network among teacher union activists in US unions. To the extent that US unions do not join with Latin American teachers' struggles against the devastation of public education enacted by governments in thrall to US-controlled agencies like the World Bank, the US unions reinforce Cuban claims that the only alternative to corrupt, capitalist plutocracies is Cuba's undemocratic social and political model. On the other hand, when Cuba's denials of elementary political rights, like the right to form an independent teachers union, are ignored, progressive activists in US teachers unions unwittingly reinforce neoliberalism's contention that "there is no alternative" way of organizing the economy and political life that allows for both economic and political democracy.

When the Cuban government greets political dissent with police action and progressives fail to support the Cuban people's right to freedoms that are exercised (though increasingly with restraints) in liberal capitalist democracies, we willy-nilly reinforce pro-capitalist and pro-US political tendencies among Cuban dissidents. The Campaign for Peace and Democracy petition of June 2003, simultaneously condemning both US threats to Cuba and Cuba's arrest of scores of people for nonviolent political activity, challenges the symbiosis between Cuba and neoliberalism that is reinforced by AFT and NEA unwillingness to support the IDEA network, as well as the IDEA network's defense of Cuban society as a progressive model. As the exchanges about repression in Cuba in previous issues of *New Politics* (most recently in volume 9, no. 3 and no. 4) reveal, the consistent defense of political freedom exemplified by the Campaign for

Peace and Democracy petition on Cuba is sometimes rejected as providing backhanded support for US imperialism. I think the embrace of Cuba at the Educational Summit and the absence of participation by US teacher union activists illustrate quite the opposite: Our ability to build an international struggle against policies that are destroying public education (as well as the quality of life generally, working conditions, the environment, et cetera) depends on projecting a vision of another world that provides both political freedom *and* social control over economic resources.

A consistent commitment to full democracy raises other urgent issues for education activists and teachers unions. Attention to gender inequality in education, including its presence in the ranks of the teachers unions' leadership throughout the hemisphere, is still a problem.

Teaching young children is very much "women's work" throughout the world, and the vast majority of teachers in the hemisphere are women. Yet on the dais of the Educational Summit opening session sat seven men and one woman—and only the men spoke. Also, special concerns in the education of and for indigenous peoples and issues of racism were muffled when they were heard at all. As the upheaval in Bolivia indicates, racism is not exclusively a US problem, yet the special issues that arise in education of the often rural communities of indigenous peoples in Latin America seemed to me not explored as fully as they ought to have been in the Educational Summit or in IDEA network publications. For teachers unions to be "close to the people," as several union representatives advocated, they must support and lead struggles to allow indigenous peoples to enjoy the material benefits of industrial societies without being forced to assimilate. Unions throughout the world, not just those of teachers, face the problem of negotiating alliances with social movements that are not based in the workplace.

At Mar del Plata I saw a movement that has possibilities to make a just world a reality. The opening rally of the contracumbre, with its passion and verve, contrasted so sharply with tired speechifying that characterizes most labor protests in the United States. Not since participating in the AFL-CIO's huge march on Washington, DC, in defense of striking PATCO workers (Professional Air Traffic Controllers Organization) who had been fired by Ronald Reagan have I seen such an impressive illustration of the power of trade unions to use their institutional strength to lead a social movement. CTERA organized a conference that brought together hundreds of teacher union activists from Latin America and Canada, aligning teacher union struggles with the demands of the contracumbre. Thulas Nxesi's participation in the Educational Summit and the People's Summit, rather than the official summit meetings, illustrated that US control of the EI has been broken. In the IDEA network, Latin American and Canadian teachers unions have developed a fledgling hemispheric umbrella organization that has exciting potential. The support the British Columbia Teachers Federation (BCTF) received when BCTF teachers went out on strike shortly before the contracumbre shows the IDEA network's potential. Teachers unions in the IDEA network sent telegrams and messages of support of the strikers to the BC government and even staged demonstrations at Canadian consulates.

Union activists from several countries agreed that we face an international challenge in bringing into union activity the generation of teachers raised in the 1980s and 1990s, periods in which conservative ideology dominated. The generation that now leads teachers unions was frequently schooled in radical politics in the 1960s and '70s. Our ability to bring into activity and leadership younger teachers who can continue and expand our project of protecting public education depends on our willingness to scrutinize teacher unionism's successes and failures.

I suggest that many of the movement's errors can be encapsulated in the notion that democracy is a luxury that we can separate from economic struggles. A consistent struggle for democracy is, in fact, essential to win the battle to protect public education. Unions that are undemocratic in their internal life are handicapped in sustaining the kind and level of activity, what one BCTF delegate described as an "organizing culture," needed to defeat the onslaught of neoliberal politicians. Failing to insist on the right of teachers to have full political rights, including the right to organize unions that are independent of state control, reinforces the powerful ideological message of the United States and its client governments that only neoliberalism can provide political freedoms and economic stability.

A consistent defense of democracy is a supremely realistic strategy—if the other world we imagine is one of full human emancipation.

12.

"Teacher Unionism Reborn"

First published in New Politics *13, no. 4, whole #52 (Winter 2012).*

In the past few years we have witnessed a demonization of teachers unions that is close to achieving its goal: destruction of the most stable and potentially powerful defender of mass public education. Teacher unionism's continued existence is imperiled—if what we define as "existence" is organizations having the legal capacity to bargain over any meaningful economic benefits and defend teachers' rights to exercise professional judgment about what to teach and how to do it.

As I explain elsewhere,[1] financial and political elites began this project forty years ago when they imposed school reform on Latin America, Africa, and Asia as a quid pro quo for economic aid. Though specifics of this global social engineering differ from one country to another, reforms have the same footprint: School funding is cut and school systems are broken up to promote privatization under the banner of "choice"; teachers and curriculum are controlled by tying pay to standardized test scores and eliminating tenure; standardized testing measures what is taught to most students, reducing content to basic math, reading, and writing. Teachers unions have been singled out for attack because throughout the world they are the most significant barriers to this project's implementation.

Rhetoric about equalizing school outcomes for groups long denied access to adequate, let alone quality, education masks the real aim of the last twenty years of reform, creating a docile workforce that receives no more than the eighth-grade education needed to compete with workers elsewhere for jobs that can be moved easily from one city, state, or country. World Bank materials lay out the assumptions seldom articulated in this country: Money educating workers beyond the level most will need wastes scarce public funding; and minimally educated workers require minimally educated teachers, whose performance can be monitored through the use of standardized testing. The newest World Bank report, *Making Schools Work*, takes the reasoning (and policy) even further, insisting that "contract teachers" who work for one-quarter of what civil service employees receive, have no benefits, no job protection, and no rights produce good enough outcomes.[2]

The attack has been fueled by right-wing foundations and advanced by Democrats and Republicans alike. The corporate media, including traditionally liberal elements, like Hollywood, the *New Yorker* and the *New York Times*, have blanketed TV, radio, and the press with bogus premises about education's relationship to the economy and the role of teachers unions in blocking much-needed change. The Obama administration substitutes educational reforms straight out of the playbook of right-wing foundations as the panacea to unemployment and poverty. When Secretary of Education Arne Duncan avers that education is the "one true path out of poverty" he displays the administration's intention to divert attention away from unemployment, health care, child hunger, and homelessness. School improvement supplants all the economic and social reforms that have, historically, been used to ameliorate poverty. Defenders of public education frequently answer these inflated claims for education with protestations that schools can do nothing to alter the fate of poor children. Unfortunately, their response serves to heighten public perceptions that school people—teachers—refuse to take responsibility for what occurs under their watch. The more accurate and politically effective response is that schools can do more and better if we have well-prepared and well-supported teachers at work in well-resourced schools, and yet, even with these conditions, schools are hostage to powerful forces that depress achievement—factors that are beyond their control. This more nuanced defense of public education and teachers undercuts one of the most difficult problems we face in defending public education, neoliberalism's exploitation of historic inequalities in education. This is especially true in the United States, where the rhetoric of the civil rights movement has been totally hijacked in defense of charter schools and improving "teacher quality" by eliminating seniority and tenure. Even the *Nation* has bought the reification of individual teacher performance as the sine qua non of school improvement.[3]

Teachers unions globally have experienced an astoundingly well-orchestrated, well-financed attack, and resistance elsewhere in the world has been forceful and persistent.[4] In contrast, US teachers unions have been easy targets. Most teachers belong to a local affiliate of the NEA or the AFT. Both the NEA and AFT are national unions with state-level organizations. In general, teachers in the largest cities are in the AFT, which is a member of the AFL-CIO. The NEA functions as a union and collaborates with labor on legislation and in politics but is not in the AFL-CIO. In the NEA, state organizations are the most powerful component. In the AFT, the local affiliate is key. Staff generally control the NEA, officers the AFT. In most school systems, the union apparatus is intact, but the organizations are shells, weakened by their embrace of the "business union" or "service model" that characterizes most US unions. The synergy of business unionism's hierarchical ethos and the legal framework giving unions the right to bargain on behalf of teachers, namely exclusive representation as bargaining agent, the right to collect an "agency fee" (payment to the union of what is generally the equivalent of dues, to cover expenses the union expends in negotiating and enforcing the contract), and dues check-off (automatic deduction of dues from the member's paycheck) has encouraged a totally bureaucratic approach to contract enforcement, member passivity, and erosion of the union's school-site presence. Local union officers and activists have often been clueless about how to respond to the blitzkrieg of vitriol, and the national unions have been little help. They have been unwilling to "rock the boat," desiring above all to stay politically moored to Obama, a president who has pressed for a thoroughly anti-teacher, anti-union, anti–public education agenda. Another factor is, of course, the personal power and privilege national officers and staff enjoy as a result of their cozy relationship with powerful elites.

From the start of mass public education, teachers unions, like most of organized labor, turned a blind eye to racism and anti-immigrant sentiment.[5] Teachers unions' failure to acknowledge this history has facilitated their being cast—incredibly, by billionaires who have plundered the nation's resources—as a special interest group, more interested in protecting teachers' jobs than in helping poor children succeed in school. Many parents and citizens, even some teachers, have been persuaded that tenure and seniority protect "dead wood," not realizing that when tenure and seniority are lost, so is democratic space in classrooms. The unions' unwillingness to acknowledge schooling's past and current role in reproducing social inequality and their reluctance to work as partners with activists to take on racism, sexism, militarization, and anti-immigrant prejudice have weakened their credibility with groups who should be teacher unionists' strongest allies.

This problem is exemplified by Diane Ravitch's defense of teacher unions. Unlike Chester Finn, a former ally who brags about his desire to destroy public education, Ravitch understands that once public education is destroyed, like Humpty Dumpty, it won't be put back together again—and when public education goes, so will a powerful force for democracy. Another explanation for Ravitch's about-face on the neoliberal reforms she advocated as part of the Bush administration is that she is an intellectual and, unlike her former neoconservative allies, is genuinely interested in education. She is, rightly, horrified by the anti-intellectualism that is writ large in neoliberalism's successful efforts to vocationalize education. Most of what she writes is eloquent, passionate, and accurate. Unlike the disoriented bureaucrats who run the unions, Ravitch understands that a fight needs to be made and she is willing to wage it. Ravitch criticized mayoral control of the New York City schools as undemocratic when the president of the union representing New York

City teachers supported the measure. Ravitch has come out against linking teacher pay to test scores while the national unions have caved. Ravitch has shown the union bureaucrats how they could, if they wished, defend the union and public education more effectively. She is Albert Shanker's doppelganger, that is, while he still acted like union president rather than a labor statesman.

However, as was the case with Shanker and is true of NEA and AFT officials today, Ravitch's defense of teacher unionism and public education is constrained by an ideological commitment to defending US capitalism at any cost. Because she can't or won't acknowledge what has been wrong with US society and public education, she can't devise a compelling alternative to the neoliberal reforms. She embeds, subtly, in her current defense of public education the claim that there was no crisis in US public education before the neoliberal reforms were imposed. But there was. The left historians she blasted in the 1960s and '70s in her defense of the status quo had it right. The schools did—and do—reproduce social inequality. In her recent essay in the *New York Review of Books* (September 29, 2011) she reduces current educational inequality between whites and minorities to yet another in a series of overblown crises US schools have endured since their creation. She argues that "poverty matters," which it does, of course. So does racism, which she does not mention. So do other forms of discrimination, which she ignores. Elsewhere, Ravitch states her desire for public education to be what she experienced in high school, in Houston, Texas.[6] (In the PBS history of US public education, Ravitch fondly recalls her days as a high school cheerleader.) But how many black and Hispanic parents will fight for a return to the status quo that barred their children from schools that served whites?

An Emerging Resistance

The nation's largest cities were home to teacher unionism's original birth and its rebirth in the 1960s. Today opposition caucuses have emerged once again in cities, where conditions have deteriorated to an extent unimaginable even a decade ago. Charter schools, as their proponents freely admit, are one of the main weapons to make school systems free of union influence. A charter school is essentially its own school district, free of district regulations—and union involvement. In most large cities, teachers unions gave up seniority in transfer when the first wave of school closings began. Now, when schools are closed because of poor test scores and replaced by charter schools, experienced teachers are often thrown into pools of "displaced teachers." They must compete for jobs with new hires who earn one-half the salary. Teacher pay now comes out of a school's budget, so many principals, especially those with little or no teaching experience themselves, prefer hiring two new teachers for the price of one more-experienced teacher. A fact little publicized by the unions is that older minority teachers face intense racism when they interview for jobs, especially with young, white principals. Readers familiar with labor history will see the dismaying parallels to "shape up" on the docks and fields, before unionization brought hiring halls and protections for older workers.

Although tenure has been dismissed as irrelevant in K–12 teaching, its importance is greater today than ever before. As principals' pay is increasingly tied to improving test scores, and the noose between teacher pay and student test scores is tightened, teachers who want to give their students a richer diet than test prep are facing the prospect of losing their jobs if they follow their moral and professional principles. Even more chilling is schools' use of corporate propaganda, obtained through seemingly trustworthy vendors, as occurred with Scholastic Books promoting a fourth-grade curriculum written by the coal industry with its perspective.[7] Even where it still exists in state law, tenure has been greatly weakened because administrators can easily give teachers spurious unsatisfactory ratings due to weakened enforcement of evaluation procedures. In many city schools, principals can and do function without any check on their power, other than what is exercised by distant officials whose only concern is test scores. Over and over one hears of teachers who have bought the anti-union propaganda that is so prevalent in the media, are too overworked and demoralized to do anything other than what they are told, or are too afraid of retribution to voice a contrary opinion. The union's presence has been so eroded and its credibility so damaged that "transforming the union" in many districts probably means building it from scratch.

At the same time, some teachers have become politicized by the vicious, unfair political attacks on their ability, character, professional authority, and economic well being. Still, they often cling to the "service model" of unionism and expect "the union" to somehow, magically, intervene. The idea that they *are* the union is slowly percolating through the ranks, and increasingly, a new generation of teacher union activists is emerging. Union renewal is taking many forms, but the most important developments from a strategic perspective are occurring in the nation's cities. Not all major cities are experiencing the kind of change that's needed. For example, in Washington, DC, a protracted, ultimately successful court challenge by a former union official who vied for the presidency did little to mobilize teachers and community. On the other hand, in the Chicago Teachers Union (CTU), a vibrant leadership, mostly new to union office, has brought their commitment to mobilize the membership, explicitly rejecting business unionism. In Milwaukee, long-time education activist Bob Peterson, a founder of the magazine *Rethinking Schools*, now heads Milwaukee's teachers union. Radical teachers who previously shunned the union now understand that they need it to protect teachers' economic rights, and like Peterson, see the union capable of fighting on a "tripod" of concerns: "bread and butter unionism . . . professional unionism . . . and social justice unionism." Peterson points to the need for truly mutual alliances, building strong relations with parents and community groups "not just to ensure adequate support for public education, but so that we as a union are also involved in improving the community."[8]

Though *Rethinking Schools* and others use the term "social justice" union, I think the idea of a "social movement" union is more useful because it addresses the need for transformation of the unions internally, especially the need for union democracy. Union democracy is a thorny issue for radicals, especially those who assume leadership of moribund organizations. "Social justice" unionism addresses the positions the union takes on various political, social, and economic issues. One temptation for radicals who take office without a mobilized base to support them is that union democracy becomes a hindrance to the union acting on a "social justice" program. On the other hand, "social movement" unionism gets at the need for empowering members, building the union from the bottom up, making the union itself a social movement. A social movement union not only endorses social justice demands in education and the society, working with social movements to further these aims, it also exists as a social movement itself, pressing as much as it can against the constraints of its being a membership organization—with the responsibility to protect its members.

The CTU is probably the most important testing ground for social movement unionism. The union is now led by activists from CORE (Caucus of Rank-and-File Educators).[9] Using new-fangled social media and old-fashioned face-to-face meetings and organizing, CORE defeated the older guard leadership loyal to the national AFT office. With scarcely a second to catch their breath, CTU's new leaders were confronted with ferocious attacks by the state and city on the contract and teachers' pensions. In gaining their political footing, the inexperienced leadership made mistakes that were both natural and damaging, for instance, trusting that state union officials would be more expert about policy decisions and allowing the local president to participate in meetings with high-ranking state officials by herself. The CTU leadership faces a stunning phalanx of opponents, ranging from Mayor Rahm Emanuel, who flaunts the prestige and support he has in the White House and from powerful "friends of labor" in the Democratic Party to Republican and Democratic state politicians, eager to destroy all public employees unions, mostly especially those representing city teachers. CTU leaders must take from the state and national union resources that are needed while simultaneously doing all that is necessary to oust these officials who impede the movement's objectives. In my opinion, CORE activists are an inspiration, heroic, and wise.

Like teachers in other cities, Los Angeles teachers face a viciously anti–teachers union mayor. But what differentiates Mayor Antonio Villaraigosa is that he parlayed his position as a staffer for the teachers union, United Teachers of Los Angeles (UTLA), and his close relationship with two of UTLA's highest-ranking officers—well-known leftists—to become a labor bigwig and then mayor. UTLA was the first teachers union in a major US city in which a reform caucus succeeded in sweeping the old guard out of office. However, only a small fraction of the membership voted in the election (and in the most recent election as well). The reformers have been in the unenviable position of responding to horrific attacks while also managing the union's bureaucratic operations, without being able to count on much support from the membership. Unfortunately, the reformers, who took office in a coalition that did not permit accountability among the factions, maintained many of the bureaucratic practices of the previous administration. The leadership's disastrous decision to support mayoral control—because their buddy was the mayor—was a function of an emphasis on playing power politics rather than addressing the union's bureaucratic functioning. In the most recent elections, a long-time activist running as an independent but aligning himself with a more conservative caucus won the presidency. At the same time, a progressive caucus, PEAC (Progressive Educators for Action), took a majority of seats on the union's board of directors. What needs to be done now—and quickly—is for leaders and activists to focus financial and human resources on reviving the union at the school site. Probably one-third of the schools, campuses as they're called, lack functioning chapters. This admittedly painstaking work of educating members that they "own" the union, to help them in organizing themselves, is inescapable. One bright spot from the reformers' victory is that UTLA's Human Rights Committee has embraced international work with Canadian and Mexican teachers unions, under the umbrella of the Trinational Coalition to Defend Public Education.[10]

Of all the teachers unions in major cities, it appears at first glance that New York's union, the United Federation of Teachers (UFT), has done the best job in protecting teachers and public schools. Many of the worst abuses teachers have suffered elsewhere have been forestalled by the union's political clout in Albany. Charter schools have not mushroomed as fast as they have elsewhere, for instance, in California. Schools being closed due to low test scores are not being auctioned off to the highest bidder, as is occurring in Los Angeles. But appearances are deceiving because while the UFT has indeed been able to protect many of the vestiges of the old system by calling in its political chips, it has done so at the expense of alienating its natural allies, insulating the bureaucracy and allowing the union to all but disappear at the school and seriously erode at the district level, where union staff may decline to provide chapter chairs with the most minimal forms of support, like meeting with principals about grievances. One estimate I've heard from a loyalist to the current leadership puts the number of schools with no functioning union chapters at far more than one-third, probably closer to three-fifths. Many teachers are too frightened to attend union meetings or even meet privately with union staff at the school site. What they may consent to do, when pressed, is to put union materials in teachers' mailboxes, but they will do so only in secret. One fine young teacher in a selective Manhattan high school touted to be "progressive" and favored by leftish parents was given "unsatisfactory" ratings by the principal for "harassing" colleagues. He put a notice in their mailboxes informing them of a get-together to discuss the school's admission policies. The chapter chair refused to help because she wanted to stay in the principal's good graces, and union staff were unwilling to be involved. Their job as they see it is to file grievances that they are sure will succeed. The UFT clearly lacks the capacity—and will—to defend its members and the schools. Some activists theorize that the union is morphing, perhaps through conscious intent, from a "service model" of unionism into a membership organization that wears the mantle of union but in fact is a provider of consumer services, like low-cost auto insurance.

Still, the UFT bosses have not yet seen a serious challenge. In the last change of rule, the crown was passed to Michael Mulgrew, who actually taught in the city schools, unlike Randi Weingarten, a lawyer who served as UFT president and is currently the AFT national president. Mulgrew's face is new, but the apparatus remains impenetrably bureaucratic and the union's politics are essentially as they were under Shanker. There is little sense from the way the union leadership presents itself or acts that teacher unionism has experienced an assault that challenges its existence. The union newspaper's coverage of school struggles—or rather lack of it—shows how little engaged the UFT is in protecting the contract, schools, or teachers, as well as how remote it is from community-based groups fighting for social justice. In the October 27, 2011, issue of the union newspaper, Michael Mulgrew's picture appeared nine times in the first eleven pages. An article applauded the success of Junior ROTC at one of the city's many racially segregated city high schools. No mention was made of the anti-militarization campaigns that are occurring elsewhere in the nation, for instance in Los Angeles, with UTLA's support. Another story informed teachers about their rights—in handling disruptive students. No mention was made of advocacy groups' work about racial discrimination in school disciplinary policies, of activists working to alter school organization and culture so that "disruptive" students are less so. Stories on charter school organizing painted a glowing picture—another victory! There was one nod to the fact that Occupy Wall Street was a few blocks away from union headquarters, a story (with a picture of Michael Mulgrew) described the union's participation in a coalition demanding no tax breaks for millionaires. But mostly the newspaper contained sentimental snapshots of teachers doing charity work. In light of the real conditions in the school system, including thousands of teachers who are paid (for now) but jobless, draconian cuts in funding felt in loss of money for supplies and class sizes that often exceed the contractual norms (not enforced), and the absence of union chapters in at least one-third of the schools, the paper's contents are almost surreal. Clearly, this is a union leadership that doesn't understand that publicity about teachers walking in support of breast cancer awareness will not suffice to defend their schools, their jobs, or their right to have a real union represent them.

The UFT's one victory in recent memory was organizing family day care workers, that is, making them union members. The UFT, in alliance with ACORN, used its political muscle to win the right to have family day care workers have union representation and have their dues deducted from their wages, which are paid by the state. An election for the bargaining agent occurred, a small fraction of the workers in the unit voted, and the UFT won the vote. While this seems to be a win-win, strengthening the union and giving exploited workers union representation, in fact the "top-down" process fails to build the resiliency union members will need to win or defend gains. Often what occurs in this kind of organizing is that shortly after the election for representation, the new members are forgotten. In this familiar scenario not limited to the UFT, union officials use the new members to strengthen their bureaucratic hold on the union apparatus. Union membership gives workers access to some protections, much needed and deserved to be sure; but especially when members are not in the majority constituency (teachers in the case of the UFT), they are trapped in a union that does little to represent them. The case of the family day care workers is especially poignant because the UFT/ACORN alliance muscled out what had been the authentic community-based organizing of family day care workers, by a Brooklyn group, Families United for Racial and Economic Equality.[11]

One bright spot in the New York City teachers union's political horizon is Teachers Unite, which is trying to bring activists on social justice in schooling together with teachers who want to see the UFT transformed.[12] Teachers Unite is small but growing. One of its most successful activities has been providing workshops on building the union at the school site, taught by teachers who are themselves chapter leaders. Teachers Unite's activity demonstrates what could be done to build the union if the UFT bureaucracy really wanted to do so. Teachers from other activist groups, including the Grassroots Education Movement (GEM), which produced a splendid video countering the misinformation in *Waiting for Superman*, are collaborating with Teachers Unite on social justice campaigns in the city schools, including helping to organize against school closings.[13] Another hopeful development is that Teachers Unite is part of a still-emerging national network of reform groups.

Occupy the Unions!

If teachers unions are to continue to exist as a meaningful form of workers' representation, members need to transform them—and fast. The future of the movement depends on activists realizing that they, not staff or officers on the state and national levels, have to be the catalysts for change. Just as there is no escape from building the union at the base, there is no getting around the hard work of developing authentic alliances with parents and community activists, coalitions that acknowledge historic inequalities and support communities in their needs, rather than being paper organizations that are dusted off when the union wants to display community support. Elected officials, from school boards to governors, are violating union contracts with impunity. Lawsuits, by themselves, the favored method of dealing with law-breaking officials, can't stop this. What can is direct action undertaken with parents and community, as the CTU has done in combating school closings in Chicago.

In contrast, the AFT and NEA national leadership pursue a strategy of cozying up to their "friends" in the Democratic Party, including President Obama. This undercuts the brave activity of many teachers battling in their schools against the policies Obama and Duncan are pushing. For instance, both national unions have accepted the use of standardized tests to judge student performance and teachers' pay, in order, they say, to stay "credible." But "credible" to whom? Certainly not teachers who risk their livelihoods by speaking out against the harm done by education having been reduced to teaching to/for the test. The president of the AFT chapter in a charter school shared with me his outrage and dismay at what occurred when he called the state union for help in dealing with the principal's demand for pay increases linked to student test scores. He was told the changes the principal demanded were official AFT policy.

In July 2011, the NEA officially endorsed Obama for president. The AFT will undoubtedly follow suit, once organized labor decides the time is right to make this commitment. Although the AFT and NEA nationally are in the Democrats' hip pocket, a different scenario might occur in local school board elections. Teachers unions are beginning to run candidates for school boards. Often local unions support candidates with the same "lesser evil" rationale the national and state unions use in endorsing Democrats. But in some places, this strategy is being challenged. Instead of electing someone, anyone, who is marginally better, teachers unions are thinking of how they might use the races as an opportunity to build support from the ground up. Campaigns for school board elections can be testing grounds for building new electoral alliances, alliances that are wholly independent of both parties, speak truth to corporate power, and advance a vision of public education that supports collaboration among schooling's constituencies. As Occupy Wall Street has demonstrated, the country is hungry for leaders who will speak out against capitalism's excesses. Neither the NEA nor AFT can provide that leadership, nor can they be partners in a movement that challenges Wall Street, as long as its top officials want the unions to be included as collaborators in maintaining US capitalism's domination of US society and the globe.

As labor researchers Mayssoun Sukarieh and Stuart Tannock explain, though the AFT supports its far-flung global operations with "high-minded rhetoric of global labor solidarity, philanthropic goodwill, and democracy promotion," the union wants most of all to further US hegemony. The AFT's international operations are vast, ranging from "Bolivia to Burma and Kenya to Kazakhstan."[14] Ironically, the AFT aims to educate teacher unionists elsewhere in the world to desert the traditions of social movement unionism that we in the United States should be learning—and imitating—here at home. Given claims by some progressives that the AFT changed with the end of the Cold War and Shanker's death, it's important to note Sukarieh and Tannock contend that the AFT "continues with its cold war legacy largely uninterrupted. Its current director of international affairs, David Dorn, was also director during the Shanker era. Rather than question, apologize for, or distance itself from any of its past international work, the AFT celebrates and explicitly claims to be continuing with this exact same line of activity.... The AFT continues to expand its international programs ... from its 1990s base in Eastern Europe to the current focus on the Middle East."[15]

The AFT and NEA rely on their size, wealth, and connections with the US government to dominate the politics of the Education International (EI), the global federation of teachers unions. There used to be significant foreign policy differences between the NEA and AFT, with the NEA being more liberal. However, those distinctions, even ephemeral, seem to have been lost. Both joined in squashing democracy at the EI conference in Capetown this past summer, where they used their control of the EI's administrative apparatus to push through a palatable (to them) resolution on Palestine and Israel. According to a conference participant with whom I spoke, AFT and NEA shocked Western European delegates with their brazen (and successful) effort to control debate and force an outcome that was more in line with US foreign policy.

Three different resolutions on Palestine and Israel were presented to the conference. One came from the EI board, another from the UK higher education union, Universities and Colleges Union, and the third from the National Union of Teachers (NUT). Operating much as the AFT leadership does at its own conventions, the

AFT and NEA maneuvered to suppress the NUT resolution, which was a forthright condemnation of Israel's actions toward Palestine. They first tried to persuade the presiding NUT officer to withdraw the resolution. This effort at intimidation failed, so they warned NUT delegates that should they persist in presenting their resolution, the AFT delegation would bolt from the conference. An NEA staffer being groomed for leadership in the EI's administrative office handled negotiations on behalf of the AFT and NEA, and ultimately, a "compromise" resolution was approved, one that dropped sharp criticism of Israeli policy. Delegates from the Middle East were enraged at the resolution and by their having been silenced in the debate.

With all of the political struggles going on in the world, with the concerted attacks against teachers unions, why did the AFT and NEA make the NUT's resolution on Palestine the main focus of their political intervention at the EI? Why would the leadership of NEA and AFT jeopardize their political legitimacy by flaunting their control over the EI's administrative apparatus? The answer is in the lopsided nature of the AFT and NEA's political compass, permanently stuck in the direction of the US government's desires. Nothing counts as much for the NEA and AFT leadership as the prerogatives of US capitalism and the government that protects it. Their political loyalties to US imperialism are seen in almost every political decision. For example, the NEA and AFT ban membership by the Chinese and Cuban unions in the EI because they are not free of government control. Fair enough, but why then permit participation of the Egyptian union—entirely controlled by the Mubarak dictatorship—until the union fell in arrears on its dues, shortly before Mubarak was overthrown? Teacher union leaders from the global South object to the contradiction between EI's professed support for free trade unions throughout the world and its, that is, the NEA and AFT's, one-sided application of criteria that coincide with the desires of the US government. Under life-and-death pressure from their own governments and fearful of further attacks by international agencies that answer to Washington, teacher unionists in Asia and Africa are understandably reluctant to challenge the AFT and NEA. Given this imbalance of power between unions in the global South and the AFT and NEA, the Western European unions have a special responsibility to fight for democracy in the EI and for consistent application of the ruler measuring whether unions are indeed "free" of government control.

When Naomi Klein spoke at Occupy Wall Street she noted that the rest of the world had been waiting for this challenge at capitalism's heart. The same is true of US teacher unionism's renaissance. Teachers and students around the globe need teachers in this country to occupy their unions. At this writing, the eyes of the world are on the courageous activists who are facing down the world's most powerful elite in downtown Manhattan. Our eyes should also be on the heroic activity of teachers moving to occupy their unions. The future of public education globally depends in great measure on them.

Notes

1. Understanding the Assault on Public Education

1. Diane Ravitch eloquently and passionately attacks many of the neoliberal reforms and acknowledges the right-wing "playbook" from which they are drawn. But she rejects the international component as a "conspiracy," for ideological reasons. I analyze her stance in chapter 11 and in my remarks on a panel "What Type of School Reform Do We Really Want?" with her, which was recorded as part of the NYU Radical Film and Lecture series on March 26, 2010; see http://blip.tv/radical-film-and-lecture-series-at-nyu/what-type-of-school-reform-do-we-really-want-3444778.

2. Mary Compton and Lois Weiner, eds., *The Global Assault on Teaching, Teachers, and Their Unions: Stories for Resistance* (New York: Palgrave Macmillan, 2008). See especially the chapters on Namibia, India, and Mexico.

3. J. Pinkney Pastrana, "Subtle Tortures of the Neo-liberal Age: Teachers, Students and the Political Economy of Schooling in Chile," *Journal for Critical Education Policy Studies* 5, no. 2 (November 2007), www.jceps.com/?pageID=article&articleID=102.

4. Susan Robertson explains the origin and rationale of neoliberal policies in her chapter in *The Global Assault*.

5. Kate Rousmaniere, "White Silence: A Racial Biography of Margaret Haley." *Equity and Excellence in Education* 34, no. 2 (2001): 7–15.

6. Ann Bastian et al., *Choosing Equality: The Case for Democratic Schooling* (Philadelphia: Temple University Press, 1986).

7. See www.loisweiner.org.

2. Protecting the Heart of Teaching

1. "Heeding Humble Voices" and "Professional Right to Inform Parents about Tests," *Intercambio*, May 2010, 5–12. www.idea-network.ca/userfiles/image/file/INTERCAMBIO%202-Ingl%C3%A9s.pdf.

2. The network of Teacher Activist Groups has affiliates in many cities: www.teacheractivistgroups.org.

3. Kenneth J. Saltman, "The Failure of Corporate School Reform: Toward a New Common School Movement," *Truthout.org*, December 5, 2011, truth-out.org/index.php?option=com_k2&view=item&id=5280:the-failure-of-corporate-school-reform-toward-a-new-common-school-movement (accessed February 7, 2012).

4. "Walker, Reagan, and Populism," "Wisconsin Labor News," *Workers Independent News* (blog), posted August 4, 2011, by WIN Production, www.laborradio.org/wisconsin/home.aspx?BlogID=1002930.

5. Juan Gonzalez, "Reverend Al Sharpton's $500G Link to Education Reform," *New York Daily News*, April 2009, http://articles.nydailynews.com/2009-04-01/news/29435670_1_national-action-network-sharpton-education-equality-project.

6. Kevin K. Kumashiro, *Bad Teacher! How Blaming Teachers Distorts the Bigger Picture* (New York: Teachers College Press, 2012).

7. *The Schools Chicago's Students Deserve*, Chicago Teachers Union website, www.ctunet.com/deserve.

8. Jean Anyon, *Radical Possibilities: Public Policy, Urban Education, and a New Social Movement* (New York: Routledge, 2005).

9. Bastian et al., *Choosing Equality*.

10. Raewyn Connell, "The Neo-liberal Parent and Schools," in George Martell, ed., *Breaking the Iron Cage: Resistance to the Schooling of Global Capitalism* (Ottawa: Our Schools/Ourselves, 2008), 175–93.

11. David Tyack, *The One Best System* (Cambridge, MA: Harvard University Press, 1974).

12. Steve Golin, *The Newark Teacher Strikes: Hopes on the Line* (New Brunswick, NJ: Rutgers University Press, 2002).

13. Geoffrey Gordon Tegnell, *Democracy in Education: A Comparative Study of the Teachers' Council Movement, 1895–1968*. Unpublished doctoral dissertation, Harvard University, Graduate School of Education, 1997.

14. M. Foster, "The Role of Community and Culture in School Reform Efforts: Examining the Views of African-American Teachers," *Educational Foundations* 8, no. 2 (Spring 1994): 5–26.

15. "Bringing Human Rights to Education with CADRE," "Education,"

National Economic and Social Rights Initiative, www.nesri.org/programs/bringing-human-rights-to-education-with-cadre.

16. Wayne J. Urban, *Gender, Race, and the National Education Association* (New York: RoutledgeFalmer, 2000).

3. Building Social Movement Teachers Unions

1. Amy Dean and Wade Rathke, "Beyond the Mutual Backscratch: A New Model for Labor Community Coalitions," *New Labor Forum* 17, no. 3 (2008): 47–56.

2. Dale Mezzacappa, "Radical District Reorganization, 64 School Closings Plan," *Notebook*, April 24, 2012, www.thenotebook.org/blog/124746/radical-district-reorganization-64-school-closings-planned; Valerie Strauss, "A Defeatist Plan to Restructure Philadelphia Public Schools," *Washington Post, Answer Sheet*, April 28, 2012, www.washingtonpost.com/blogs/answer-sheet/post/a-defeatist-plan-to-restructure-philadelphia-public-schools/2012/04/28/gIQAjRSanT_blog.html.

3. Diane Ravitch has been one of the most articulate critics of privatization, and her interview in the *Economist* makes the case against her former allies in remaking US schools. See "Seven Questions for Diane Ravitch," *Democracy in America, Economist.com*, March 29, 2010, posted by R. M., www.economist.com/blogs/democracyinamerica/2010/03/education_reform_0. However, Ravitch fuses her defense of public education with a denial of schooling's inequalities. As I explain elsewhere, teachers unions can't turn back this onslaught unless we are honest about schooling's past and present inequalities, which Ravitch's love affair with US capitalism prohibits her from doing.

4. Research done elsewhere in the world describes how teachers internalize criticisms that they are not measuring up. A fine source for studies about this issue and much else about teachers' work and teachers unions throughout the world is the AERA Teachers' Work/Teacher Unions SIG blog, http://aeratwtusig.blogs.lincoln.ac.uk/.

5. Chapters 17, 18, and 25 in *The Global Assault on Teaching, Teachers, and Their Unions* describe internal struggles in unions about racism and homophobia.

6. Mario Novelli, "Globalisations, Social Movement Unionism and New Internationalisms: The Role of Strategic Learning in the Transformation of the Municipal Workers Union of EMCALI," *Globalisation, Societies and Education* 2 (July 2004): 161–90.

7. David Ost, "The Weakness of Strong Social Movements: Models of Unionism in the East European Context," *European Journal of Industrial Relations* 8, no. 1 (March 2002): 33–51.

8. Stanley Aronowitz, "No-Strike Clauses Hold Back Unions," *Labor Notes*, December 13, 2011, http://labornotes.org/blogs/2011/12/no-strike-clauses -hold-back-unions.

9. David C. Lier and Kristian Stokke, "Maximum Working-Class Unity? Challenges to Local Social Movement Unionism in Cape Town," *Antipode* 38, no. 4 (September 2006): 802–824.

10. "Too old to work—and too young to die," as the old labor song goes, performed in this YouTube video by the Vigilantes: www.youtube.com/ watch?v=JcVNbD0Vm2g.

4. The New Landscape

1. Novelli, "Social Movement Unionism," 161–90.

2. See the Labor Notes website at http://labornotes.org.

3. See the New Labor Forum site at http://newlaborforum.cuny.edu.

4. See the Association for Union Democracy site at www.uniondemocracy.org.

5. See her website at www.teachersolidarity.com.

6. See the Trinational Coalition to Defend Public Education website at www.trinational-usa.org.

7. Charter schools are called "academies" in the United Kingdom, and the organization leading the battle against them is the Anti-Academies Alliance: http://antiacademies.org.uk.

8. See the BCTF website at http://bctf.ca/socialjustice.aspx?id=6160.

9. I discuss relations with Latin American unions in chapter 10 of this book and the challenges of building an international movement in chapter 27 in *The Global Assault on Teaching*.

10. Nel Noddings, "A Morally Defensible Mission for Schools in the 21st Century," in Evans Clinchy, ed., *Transforming Public Education: A New Course for America's Future* (New York: Teachers College Press, 1997), 27– 37, http://edweb.sdsu.edu/people/Dkitchen/TE652/noddings.htm.

11. Stanley Aronowitz, "One, Two, Many Madisons: The War on Public Sector Workers," *New Labor Forum* 20, no. 2 (Spring 2011): 14–21.

5. Teacher Unionism 101

1. See *Conducting Local Union Officer Elections: A Guide for Election Officials* (Washington, DC: US Department of Labor, Office of Labor-Management Standards, 2010), www.dol.gov/olms/regs/compliance/localelec/localelec.pdf.
2. See the AUD website at www.uniondemocracy.org.
3. See the Labor Notes website at http://labornotes.org.

6. Introduction

1. Lois Weiner, "Albert Shanker's Legacy: A Critical Obituary," paper presented to the American Educational Research Association, 1998 (ERIC #ED 419 805); Lois Weiner, "Albert Shanker's Legacy," *Contemporary Education* 69, no. 4 (1998): 196–201.
2. Marjorie Murphy, *Blackboard Unions* (Ithaca, NY: Cornell University Press, 1990).
3. Vera Pavone and Norm Scott, "Albert Shanker: Ruthless Neo-Con." Review of *Tough Liberal: Albert Shanker and the Battles Over Schools, Unions, Race, and Democracy*, by Richard D. Kahlenberg (New York: Columbia University Press, 2007) in *New Politics* 45, no. 1 (2010), http://nova.wpunj.edu/newpolitics/issue45/Pavone-Scott45.htm.
4. Maurice R. Berube, *Teacher Politics: The Influence of Unions* (New York: Greenwood Press, 1988).
5. Julius Jacobson, "The Two Deaths of Max Shachtman," *New Politics* 10, no. 3 (1973): 96–99.
6. Lois Weiner, "Nitpicking: An Exploration of the Marginalization of Gender Equity in Urban School Research and Reform," *Urban Review* 34, no. 4 (2002): 363–80.

8. "Democratizing the Schools"

1. *New York Times*, October 20, 1986.
2. Chester E. Finn, Jr., Diane Ravitch, Robert T. Fancher, *Against Mediocrity* (New York: Holmes & Meier, 1984).
3. In one of her recent efforts to elevate educational standards, Ravitch, a historian of education, has advocated replacing the social studies curriculum, which often includes economics, psychology, sociology, or a survey of world cultures, with traditional history courses taught chronologically. Her own

child, who attended one of New York's elite private schools, had quite a different introduction to the social sciences from the one she is pressing the public schools to adopt. In a seminar of hers in which I was enrolled, she lamented that rather than studying history her son was asked to empty his pockets, examining and analyzing the contents, to complete some original research in cultural anthropology. Similarly, according to an article in an education supplement of the *New York Times*, Chester Finn, her collaborator at the US Education Department, sends one of his children to Phillips Exeter Academy, where James Moffett, one of the most thoughtful and influential reformers of the English curriculum in the last twenty years, did his seminal work. Ironically, while Ravitch and Finn are in a position to influence the curriculum in public schools that their children do not attend, their ideological incursions into pedagogy are resisted by the prestigious private schools to which they send their children.

4.   Ernest Boyer, *High School: A Report on Secondary Education in America* (Carnegie Foundation for the Advancement of Teaching, 1983).

5.   Theodore Sizer, *Horace's Compromise: The Dilemma of the American High School* (Boston: Houghton-Mifflin, 1984).

6.   Ann Bastian, Norm Fruchter, Marilyn Gittell, Colin Gree, and Kenneth Haskins *Choosing Equality: The Case for Democratic Schooling*, a report of the New World Foundation, soon to be released by Temple University Press.

7.   Ibid., 79.

8.   *New York Times*, December 4, 1986.

9.   In my exchange with Albert Shanker, then president of the UFT, over democracy in the union, Shanker concluded a defense of union practices with the charge that "the vast majority of opposition comes out of groups that opposed the first UFT strike in 1960 and have scabbed in others." (Issue #46 of *Union Democracy Review*, May 1985). This statement revealed his real viewpoint: anyone who disagrees with him is a scab. He and his caucus have done a thorough job of carrying out this perspective by making sure that no one who is intellectually or politically independent is appointed to any position, even pedagogical, which the union controls. In the 1985 union election, teachers in the high schools swept Shanker's caucus out of office, replacing them with the same opposition slate Shanker dismissed as scabs.

10. *Nation*, May 24, 1986.

11. *New York Teacher*, June 9, 1986.

12. Extensive research has demonstrated that the standardized reading tests given in most school systems are useless except as measurement of the

student's ability to take a standardized reading test. One alternative that is a more reliable and practical indication of a student's reading ability is an inventory of books and articles a child has demonstrated he or she can read and understand. This type of evaluation does not rank students against each other and will not yield a numerical or statistical profile of achievement, so it does not qualify as legitimate testing as the public has been taught to define it. Furthermore, it requires an agreement between school, teacher, and parent about what can and should be taught and what constitutes real literacy, so it can only be used when parents are involved in the life of the school.

13. Albert Shanker, "Where We Stand," *New York Times*, June 1, 1986.

14. *American Educator*, June 1985.

15. Perhaps the best recent history of public education, one that obviously influenced *Choosing Equality*, is *The One Best System*, by David Tyack (Harvard University Press, 1974), a history of American urban education which argues that "The search for the one best system has ill-served the pluralistic character of American society" (page 11). Tyack also criticizes the "animus against the lower-middle class teacher" as "uncharitable and insidious" and points out that historically one of the chief reasons for the failure of educational reform has been the demand for a "change of philosophy or tactics on the part of the individual school employee rather than systemic change—and concurrent transformations in the distribution of power and wealth in the society as a whole" (page 10).

10. "Neoliberalism, Teacher Unionism, and the Future of Public Education"

1. In my identification of the neoliberal agenda, I use a definition of Roberto Unger, employed by several educational researchers in Europe investigating global changes in education. Unger defines neoliberalism as an economic program (not just a collection of disparate policies) with these characteristics: fiscal balance, which is achieved primarily through limits to public spending rather than by increases in monies received through taxation; heightened integration into the world trading system and its existing rules; privatization of services, which includes adoption of Western laws of private property; acceptance of some social safety nets to ameliorate inequality resulting from other aspects of the program.

2. See econ.worldbank.org/files/23475_GCE_response_to_WDR.pdf. The final version is at econ. worldbank.org/wdr/wdr2004/text_30023.

3.   See www.indymedia.org.uk/en/regions/cambridge/2004/02/286118.html.
4.   See Paul Buhle's obituary for Shanker in *New Politics* 6, no. 3 (new series), whole no. 23, Summer 1997, http://nova.wpunj.edu/newpolitics/issue23/buhle23.htm, or "Albert Shanker's Legacy," *Contemporary Education* 69, no. 4 (summer 1998).
5.   Fred van Leeuwen, "Remarks at EI Third World Congress," www.ei_ie.org/congress2001/index.htm.
6.   Kim Scipes's May 2002 "AFL-CIO and Venezuela: Return of Labor Imperialism, or a Mistaken Reaction?" on the AFL-CIO involvement in Venezuela, sent on the ZNet message board, usefully describes the AFT's involvement on the wrong side of popular struggles against dictatorships, http://mobile.zcommunications.org/afl-cio-and-venezuela-return-of-labor-imperialism-or-a-mistaken-reaction-by-kim-scipes.
7.   econ.worldbank.org/files/23475_GCE_response_to_WDR.pdf.
8.   www.tuac.org/statemen/communiq/StMinEduc2004eDublinWHP.pdf.
9.   www.ei_ie.org/pub/english/tradeducation/tradeducation_02_e.pdf.
10.   "Initial Ideas About Motivation and Framework from the Director & Co-Director of the WDR, August 21, 2002" is part of the consultation process for the 2004 World Development Report *Making Services Work for Poor People*. As of August 1, 2012, the document could be found at http://siteresources.worldbank.org/INTWDR2004/Resources/17976_ReinikkaShantaInitialFramework.pdf. For the final WDR report, go to http://wdronline.worldbank.org/worldbank/a/c.html/world_development_report_2004/abstract/WB.0-8213-5468-X.abstract.
      The World Bank has shifted the URLs for the initial framework many times since the article was first published. The easiest way to locate it is to go to the World Bank website and find the list of documents in the consultations resulting in the final version of *Making Services Work for Poor People*. Readers who want a copy of the report can contact me directly as I have saved the file. The EI has also taken down its response to the initial report, and to my knowledge, it is no longer available.
11.   See the BCTF website at bctf.ca/social/globalization.

11. "The (People's) Summit of the Americas"

1.   Lois Weiner, "A Special New Politics Symposium: NCLB: A Progressive Response," *New Politics* 10, no. 2 (Winter 2005), http://newpol.org/node/279.
2.   Available from Corrugated Films; see www.corrugate.org.
3.   http://americas.irc_online.org/borderlines/1995/b114/b114foc_body.html.

12. "Teacher Unionism Reborn"

1. Lois Weiner, "Neoliberalism, Teacher Unionism, and the Future of Public Education," *New Politics* 10, no. 2, www.newpol.org/print/node/285.

2. World Bank, *Making Schools Work*, http://siteresources.worldbank.org/EDUCATION/Resources/278200-1298568319076/makingschools work.pdf.

3. See Lois Weiner, "Matt Damon, Diane Ravitch, and Scapegoating Teachers," *New Politics*, August 6, (2011), http://www.newpol.org/node/497.

4. The *Teacher Solidarity* blog at www.teachersolidarity.com is probably the best source of information about teacher union resistance globally.

5. K. Rousmaniere, "White Silence: A Racial Biography of Margaret Haley," *Equity and Excellence in Education* 34, no. 2 (2001): 7–15.

6. See Lois Weiner, "What's Right—and Wrong—in Diane Ravitch's New Take on School Reform," *New Politics*, April 11, 2010, http://www.newpol.org/node/292.

7. See Tell Scholastic: Stop Selling Kids on Coal. Note: The campaign was successful and the link is no longer active.

8. Bob Peterson, "It's Time to Re-imagine and Reinvent the MTEA," MTEA Convocation, Milwaukee, WI, September 21, 2011, http://www.mtea.org/Public/pdf/Re-imaginespeech.pdf.

9. See the CORE website at www.coreteachers.com.

10. See the Trinational Coalition to Defend Public Education's website at www.trinational-usa.org.

11. See the Families United for Racial and Economic Equality website at www.old.furee.org.

12. See the Teachers Unite website at www.teachersunite.net.

13. See, for example, "Inconvenient Truth Screening @NYU Oct 27th," GEM NYC blog, posted by Grassroots Education Movement, October 21, 2011, http://gemnyc.org/2011/10/21/inconvenient-truth-screening-nyu-oct-27th.

14. Mayssoun Sukarieh and Stuart Tannock, "The American Federation of Teachers in the Middle East: Teacher Training as Labor Imperialism," *Labor Studies Journal* 35, no. 2 (June 2010): 181–97, doi:10.1177/0160449X08325993

15. Ibid., 186.

Selected References

Anyon, Jean. *Radical Possibilities: Public Policy, Urban Education, and a New Social Movement.* New York: Routledge, 2005.

Aronowitz, Stanley. "One, Two, Many Madisons: The War on Public Sector Workers." *New Labor Forum* 20, no. 2 (Spring 2011): 14–21.

Bastian, Ann, Norm Fruchter, Marilyn Gittell, Colin Greer, and Kenneth Haskins. *Choosing Equality: The Case for Democratic Schooling.* Philadelphia: Temple University Press, 1986.

Berube, Maurice R. *Teacher Politics: The Influence of Unions.* New York: Greenwood Press, 1988.

Compton, Mary and Lois Weiner, eds. *The Global Assault on Teaching, Teachers, and Their Unions: Stories for Resistance.* New York: Palgrave Macmillan, 2008.

Connell, Raewyn. "The Neo-liberal Parent and Schools." In Hugo Aboites et al., *Breaking the Iron Cage: Resistance to the Schooling of Global Capitalism.* Ottawa: Our Schools/Ourselves (2008): 175–93.

Foster, Michelle. "The Role of Community and Culture in School Reform Efforts: Examining the Views of African-American Teachers." *Educational Foundations* 8, no. 2 (Spring 1994): 5–26.

Golin, Steve. *The Newark Teacher Strikes: Hopes on the Line.* New Brunswick, NJ: Rutgers University Press, 2002.

Jacobson, Julius. "The Two Deaths of Max Shachtman," *New Politics* 10, no. 3 (1973): 96–99.

Kumashiro, Kevin K. *Bad Teacher! How Blaming Teachers Distorts the Bigger Picture.* New York: Teachers College Press, 2012.

Lier, David C. and Kristian Stokke. "Maximum Working-Class Unity? Challenges to Local Social Movement Unionism in Cape Town." *Antipode* 38, no. 4 (September 2006): 802–824.

Murphy, Marjorie. *Blackboard Unions*. Ithaca, NY: Cornell University Press, 1990.

Novelli, Mario. "Globalisations, Social Movement Unionism and New Internationalisms: The Role of Strategic Learning in the Transformation of the Municipal Workers Union of EMCALI." *Globalisation, Societies and Education* 2 (July 2004): 161–90.

Ost, David. "The Weakness of Strong Social Movements: Models of Unionism in the East European Context." *European Journal of Industrial Relations* 8, no. 1 (March 2002): 33–51.

Pavone, Vera and Scott, Norm. "Albert Shanker: Ruthless Neo-Con." Review of *Tough Liberal: Albert Shanker and the Battles Over Schools, Unions, Race, and Democracy*, by Richard D. Kahlenberg. New York: Columbia University Press, 2007. In *New Politics* 45, no. 1 (2010). http://nova.wpunj.edu/newpolitics/issue45/Pavone-Scott45.htm.

Rousmaniere, Kate. "White Silence: A Racial Biography of Margaret Haley." *Equity and Excellence in Education* 34, no. 2 (2001): 7–15.

Saltman, Kenneth J. "The Failure of Corporate School Reform: Toward a New Common School Movement." December 5, 2011, available: http://truth-out.org/index.php?option=com_k2&view=item&id=5280:the-failure-of-corporate-school-reform-toward-a-new-common-school-movement (accessed February 7, 2012).

Tegnell, Geoffrey. *Democracy in Education: A Comparative Study of the Teachers' Council Movement, 1895–1968*. Unpublished doctoral dissertation, Harvard University, Graduate School of Education, 1997.

Tyack, David. *The One Best System*. Cambridge, MA: Harvard University Press, 1974.

Urban, Wayne. J. *Gender, Race, and the National Education Association*. New York: RoutledgeFalmer, 2000.

Weiner, Lois. "Albert Shanker's Legacy: A Critical Obituary." Paper presented to the American Educational Research Association, 1998. (ERIC #ED 419 805).

———. "Albert Shanker's Legacy." *Contemporary Education* 69, no. 4 (1998): 196–201.

———. "Nitpicking: An Exploration of the Marginalization of Gender Equity in Urban School Research and Reform." *Urban Review* 34, no. 4 (2002): 363–80.

———. "Teacher Unionism Reborn." *New Politics* 13, no. 4 (Winter 2012): 56–78.

———. *Urban Teaching: The Essentials*, 2nd edition. New York: Teachers College Press, 2003.

Index

About Haymarket Books

Haymarket Books is a nonprofit, progressive book distributor and publisher, a project of the Center for Economic Research and Social Change. We believe that activists need to take ideas, history, and politics into the many struggles for social justice today. Learning the lessons of past victories, as well as defeats, can arm a new generation of fighters for a better world. As Karl Marx said, "The philosophers have merely interpreted the world; the point, however, is to change it."

We take inspiration and courage from our namesakes, the Haymarket Martyrs, who gave their lives fighting for a better world. Their 1886 struggle for the eight-hour day reminds workers around the world that ordinary people can organize and struggle for their own liberation.

For more information and to shop our complete catalog of titles, visit us online at www.haymarketbooks.org.

Also from Haymarket Books

Autoworkers Under the Gun
A Shop-Floor View of the End of the American Dream• Gregg Shotwell, Foreword by Jerry Tucker

The Civil Wars in U.S. Labor
Birth of a New Workers' Movement or Death Throes of the Old? • Steve Early

Education and Capitalism
Struggles for Learning and Liberation • Edited by Jeff Bale and Sarah Knopp

Schooling in Capitalist America
Educational Reform and the Contradictions of Economic Life • Samuel Bowles and Herbert Gintis

About the Author

Lois Weiner began her career in education as a high school teacher of English, journalism, and home economics, and for fifteen years taught in public schools in California, suburbs of New York, and New York City itself. After receiving her doctorate from Harvard Graduate School of Education, she began teaching education at New Jersey City University, where she now coordinates a graduate program for experienced urban teachers.

Her first book, *Preparing Teachers for Urban School*, was honored by the American Educational Research Association (AERA) for its contribution to research on teacher education. To bring her research to a wider audience, Dr. Weiner wrote *Urban Teaching: The Essentials*, which has been called a "classic" and is used in programs of teacher education throughout the United States and Canada. She is the author of dozens of articles on urban teaching and school reform and is well-known in teacher education as a scholar/activist committed to social justice.

A life-long teacher union activist, she has served as an officer of three different union locals. She served as president of the AERA Special Interest Group on teachers' work and teachers unions. She and Mary Compton coedited a pathbreaking collection of essays, *The Global Assault on Teaching, Teachers, and Their Unions: Stories for Resistance*. The book is unique in combining an international perspective on the attacks on public education with analysis about the role of teachers unions in developing global resistance.

Professor Weiner completed her undergraduate studies at the University of California, Berkeley, and the University of Stockholm, Sweden and received her MA from Teachers College, Columbia University. She is a member of the editorial board of *New Politics*, for which she blogs on education and politics.